Douglas
Jetliners

Guy Norris and Mark Wagner

MBI Publishing Company

First published in 1999 by MBI Publishing Company, PO Box 1, 729 Prospect Avenue, Osceola, WI 54020-0001 USA

MBI Publishing Company books are also available at discounts in bulk quantity for industrial or sales-promotional use. For details write to Special Sales Manager at Motorbooks International Wholesalers & Distributors, 729 Prospect Avenue, PO Box 1, Osceola, WI 54020-0001 USA.

Library of Congress Cataloging-in-Publication Data

Norris, Guy
    Douglas Jetliners / Guy Norris and Mark Wagner.
        p. cm. -- (Enthusiast color series)
    Includes index.
    ISBN 0-7603-0676-1 (pbk. : alk. paper)
    1. Douglas airplanes--History. I. Wagner, Mark. II. Title. III. Series.
  TL686.D65N67 1999
  629.133'349--dc21   98-53250

On the front cover: A United DC-8-71 makes an impressive spectacle as it soars overhead on finals for Las Vegas McCarran International in 1989. United was the largest single customer for the CFM56 engine conversion program. In fact, the airline effectively launched the program in 1979 by having all 29 members of its Series 61 fleet re-engined by Cammacorp, in a deal worth $400 million.

On the frontispiece: A close-up view of one of Emery Worldwide's DC-8s. Venerable DC-8 freighters form the backbone of Emery's fleet, which includes more than 40 of the type. These aircraft are frequently seen operating out of Dayton International Airport in Ohio. This Emery hub is strategically located within 90 minutes reach of nearly 78 percent of the United States and 55 percent of the principal business centers in Canada. It also serves as one of the company's eight international gateways to 229 countries overseas.

On the title page: Externally identical to its MD-82 sisters, this Delta MD-88 is equipped with an electronic flight instrument system (EFIS), or "glass cockpit." This system change and others, including a redesigned interior, were significant enough to warrant adoption of the MD-88 designation.

On the back cover: With flaps and slats deployed, a Hawaiian Airlines DC-10-10 powers in on final to Los Angeles International. The Honolulu-based airline operates its DC-10-10s from the islands into cities like Los Angeles, San Francisco, and Seattle bringing cargo and passengers to and from the mainland United States.

Edited by Michael Haenggi
Designed by Dan Perry

Printed in Hong Kong

CONTENTS

ACKNOWLEDGMENTS

Thanks to the many Boeing and former Douglas employees who helped bring this project to life. Led by the able John Thom, they include Warren Lamb, Barbara Raines, Bob Saling, and naturally, Don Hanson who retired in 1998. Thanks also to Sean Griffin, Mike Lombardi, and Tom Lubbesmeyer. In addition we would like to thank John Bailey, Paul Barker, Austin Brown, Anthony Concil, Tim Crows, Tracey Deakin, John Ajax Dekker, Andrew Dizz Delaney, Mike Delaney, Bruce Drum, Robert L. Frelow, Ken Graeb, Robert Grundy, Capt Ian Johnson, Chris Kjelgaard, Kensuke Kotera, Capt. Mike Kruger, Hideaki Kuroki, John A. Lewandowski, Capt. Mike Livesey, Michael Marek, Andy Marsh, Andy and Ali Maynard, Rosie Moore, Dave "DAC" Ruck, Justin Russell, Hiroshi Sakatsume, Naoya Sato, Lord and Lady Scantlebury, A.A. Scheel, Hiroshi Shimada, Andy Smith, Tetsuhisa Sugano, Katsuhiko Yumino, Katherine Ward, and Capt. Ali Wells. Thanks to Allan Winn, Carol Reed, and the team of Flight International magazine, Judy, Greg and Tom for endless patience, and a big thank you, as always, to our editor Mike Haenggi.

Guy Norris—Los Angeles-based West Coast Editor of Flight International magazine.
Mark Wagner—Pilot and Chief Photographer of Flight International magazine based out of London, UK.

INTRODUCTION

Almost 3,500 Douglas-built jetliners have been produced, the majority of which are still providing valuable daily service around the world. Here, a busy evening scene at Seatac International Airport in 1998 reveals three generations of Douglas products. An Alaska Airlines MD-83 takes off in front of a Northwest DC-10 and several DC-8 freighters.

In August 1998, the famous name of Douglas Aircraft disappeared forever. The change seemed inevitable following Boeing's takeover of McDonnell Douglas the previous year. For a while, Boeing maintained the Douglas name by referring to its newly acquired Long Beach site as the Douglas Products Division. However, with the ensuing decision to close all indigenous aircraft production lines (apart from the MD-95, which was renamed the 717), the divisional title became irrelevant.

The closure of the MD-80/90 twinjet lines in 2000 and final deliveries from the MD-11 trijet line in 2001 marks the end of an era in aviation history. The era goes all the way back to Donald Douglas' first commercial airliner, the DC-1, introduced in 1933. The surviving product, the diminutive 717, is the sole remnant of the DC line as the company moves into the twenty-first century. However, it is accompanied by thousands of existing Long Beach products whose rugged construction and fine design ensure that the Douglas legacy will remain a vibrant force for years to come.

—Guy Norris

I

DC-8: LONG-RANGE PIONEER

The date was May 30, 1958. The four-engine jetliner stood poised for takeoff at the end of the newly extended, 10,000-foot runway at Long Beach Municipal Airport. With a banshee-like scream, the four Pratt & Whitney JT3C turbojets achieved maximum thrust as Douglas chief test pilot A. G. "Heimie" Heimerdinger released the brakes.

Trailing a black cloud of exhaust smoke, the DC-8 quickly reached its rotation speed of 128 knots. After roaring down 3,250 feet of runway, the aircraft soared into the air, cheered on by a crowd of 95,000 Douglas workers and their families. For the Douglas Aircraft Company (DAC), it marked the start of a new era that would eventually lead to the production of more than 3,500 jetliners—roughly 30 percent of all Western-built civil jet aircraft manufactured by the late 1990s.

The first flight was the culmination of events that had begun six years earlier, when a DC-8 project office was set up at the company's Santa Monica headquarters. The project was tailored initially to a 1952 U.S. Air Force requirement for a jet-powered, airborne tanker with a maximum takeoff weight of approximately 250,000 pounds. The aircraft was expected to perform at roughly the same speed and altitude as the Boeing B-47 Stratojet and the newly introduced B-52 bomber. The introduction of the revolutionary, swept-wing B-47 had quickly rendered the sluggish, propeller-driven KC-97 tankers obsolete.

The USAF requirement was an urgent product of the Cold War, but it also provided a ready-made blueprint for America's first commercial jet transport. The tanker/transport project offered the U.S. aviation industry a chance to catch up with the British, who were leading the race to develop a jet transport with the de Havilland Comet. The British were not alone; the ambitious Avro Canada C. 102 Jetliner had been flown for the first time in August of 1949, just two weeks after the Comet's debut. The Soviets were busy developing a civil version of the Tupolev Tu-16 bomber, which eventually became the Tu-104. The French, too, were drawing up plans for a short-haul airliner. In September of 1952, the French launched the X-210 project, which ultimately led to the Sud-Aviation Caravelle.

However, despite the positive omens and the promising market, the leap to jet transports was not an easy one for Douglas. Unlike Boeing, which had not done very well commercially with its Model 377 Stratocruiser, Douglas had enjoyed up to 70 percent of the civil airliner market with a string of piston-powered Douglas Commercial (DC) aircraft. Thanks to its transport heritage,

The distinctive ram-air intakes of the DC-8's air-conditioning system loom large as this UPS aircraft nears touchdown. Established in 1988, UPS is now the world's largest package-delivery service. Their fleet consists of over 200 aircraft, including 23 DC-8-71Fs and 26 DC-8-73Fs.

The DC-8's approach speed was only a few knots higher than that of the DC-7, a design goal achieved by using a modest, 30-degree wing sweep angle and large flaps. Here an elderly DC-8-52, originally delivered to United in 1965, makes another landing for Faucett. The Peruvian carrier finally retired this trusty aircraft, named *Santa Isabel*, in 1992. The DC-8 had amassed almost 54,000 hours of service.

established with the DC-3/C-47 and later the DC-4/C-54, the company had developed the best-selling DC-6, DC-6A, and DC-6B. At the insistence of American Airlines chairman C. R. Smith, it then developed a "stretched" version to compete with the improved and faster variants of its main competitor, the Lockheed Constellation. In all, Douglas built 704 variants (civil and military) of the DC-6 and 338 variants of the DC-7. The company dominated the fledgling postwar airline industry with the DC-7.

The DC-7 extended the life of the company's piston-powered product line until 1958, but it also delayed the launch of the DC-8 by as much as one year. In turn, this delay created both good and bad news for Douglas. The good news was that, as a "paper plane," the DC-8 design could easily be altered to meet the challenge posed by a new Boeing design called the 707. When airlines complained about the 707 design, Douglas could simply widen the fuselage or increase the range of its conceptual plane in response. Boeing, on the other hand, faced huge redesign costs. The bad news for Douglas was that the 707 enjoyed an unassalable lead in the marketplace and ultimately doubled the sales of the DC-8.

Family Plan

By 1953, Douglas had arrived at the baseline DC-8 design. The basic aircraft had a 130-foot span wing, which was swept back by 30 degrees and supported four jets in pods beneath the wing. Although the DAC design team had studied hundreds of alternatives, including aircraft like the Comet with engines mounted inside the wing root, the podded design worked best. It allowed

A Rolls-Royce Conway-powered DC-8, similar to this rare ex-Alitalia Series 43, achieved fame in August 1961. It became the first commercial jetliner to exceed the speed of sound. The milestone was passed while a test team was verifying the performance of a leading edge improvement in an aircraft destined for Canadian Pacific. Over the Edwards Air Force Base test range in California, the DC-8 dived from 52,000 feet. It achieved a top speed of 660.6 miles per hour (Mach 1.012) at 41,088 feet.

The emergence of the DC-8 Jet Trader helped stimulate sales at a critical time for Douglas. One of the first to be delivered was this DC-8-54JT (line number 207), now classed a -55F. Handed over to Seaboard World Airlines in June 1964, it passed through several owners including the French Air Force before entering service with MK Airlines, a UK-based company. It is pictured on a low-level photo sortie over the stormy English Channel.

A rather battered Andes-operated DC-8-53F loads up with cargo for the return flight to Ecuador. Originally operated by Japan Air Lines for 17 years, the aircraft would probably have ended up in the breakers yard like many of its contemporaries had it not been converted to a freighter in 1981. The relatively low acquisition costs and a large, 85-inch by 140-inch cargo door ensured a new lease on life as a profitable freighter well into the 1990s.

the plane to carry more fuel in the wing; it was good for maintenance by allowing easy access to the engines at a time when they were basically unreliable; and it provided bending relief moment for the wing structure, which could be made lighter as a result.

The main undercarriage consisted of two main units, each with four wheels mounted on a common axis, and a conventional nose gear unit. The main wheels pivoted 90 degrees before retracting into the lower fuselage at the wing root. The fuselage itself was designed around a "double-bubble" cross section that allowed six-across seating in a 132-inch-wide main cabin. By making the "bubbles" into two circular arcs of different radii, the

design team produced a low-drag cross section. The fuselage provided adequate space for the passenger cabin and a lower cargo hold that was big enough to stand up in.

Right from the start, the company intended to offer the DC-8 in two versions. The baseline domestic version, the DC-8A, seated up to 80 people and was powered by four Pratt & Whitney J57 turbojets. These engines were later known as JT3s. The externally identical DC-8B, or international version, seated 76 people in a standard configuration. It was powered by the J75, later known as the JT4.

Despite the blow of losing the USAF tanker competition to Boeing in February 1955, Douglas

A DC-8-55F Jet Trader powers into the air on yet another mission. The fully convertible version could carry a 91,000-pound payload. The dedicated freighter, purchased only by United, offered a capacity of up to 96,000 pounds. The JT concept emerged partly from attempts by Douglas to attract USAF interest in a utility transport. The version took advantage of the much greater lift capacity of the Series 50, which came with wing and engine improvements.

decided to move forward with the DC-8, announcing the new plane as a private venture on June 7, 1955. Development costs were estimated at $450 million, and the first flight was scheduled for 1957. By now, the aircraft was starting to grow. Its span was up to 134 feet, 6 inches. Its length had increased to 140 feet, 6 inches, allowing the DC-8 to accommodate 125 passengers.

The first big sales breakthrough came on October 13, 1955, when Pan American announced orders for 25 JT4-powered international DC-8s and 20 Boeing 707s. Pan Am preferred the larger cross section of the DC-8, but it was forced to order the 707 because of its earlier availability. By the time Pan Am placed its order, the 707 prototype had been flying for 15 months; the factory in which the DC-8 would be assembled had not even been built. Encouraged by Pan Am's lead, other airlines rushed to place orders. By the end of the year, eight airlines had booked places for 99 aircraft.

The design was further refined throughout 1956, and the aircraft grew again. Its span increased to 139 feet, 9 inches with a 5-foot root insert. The fuselage grew to 148 feet, 10 inches, allowing room for 19 additional passengers. The extra root area increased fuel capacity by 20,000 pounds, an enhancement that was to prove crucial to the long-term success of the program. The fuselage was also due to grow to 150 feet, 6 inches before final assembly, and the main gear was reconfigured to the more conventional, four-wheeled bogie arrangement.

More orders arrived. Trans-Canada became the first to order four of a Rolls-Royce Conway-powered version, later dubbed the Series 40. By the end of the year, sales had climbed to 122. The total had reached 133 by May 1958, just 17 fewer than sales for the 707, which had enjoyed a significant head start.

Construction began with the milling of the first spar cap in September 1956, but the aircraft did not take shape until October of the following year, when the wings were joined to the fuselage. The mating took place in a huge new $20 million

Delivered in 1969 as United's Mainliner *Hilo Hattie*, this DC-8-62 continued its link with the Pacific Islands when Hawaiian Airlines began leasing it in 1985. Here it is prepared for its long return journey from Zurich to Honolulu. Note the sharply forward-raked engine pylons, which were redesigned to project from under the larger wing rather than impinging on the leading edge. The engines hung 40 inches farther forward as a result, reducing interference with the wing and improving cruise efficiency by a staggering 8.5 percent over the DC-8-50.

facility, where ground had been broken during the previous April. The 1.1 million-square-foot site, consisting of two main assembly buildings, was completed in just 13 months. The company immediately transferred skilled staff to the facility from Santa Monica's Clover Field, home of Douglas from the earliest years through the DC-7 era.

The first aircraft, dubbed Ship One, was rolled out on April 9, 1958, and made its maiden flight seven weeks later on May 30. It was joined in the test program by Ship Two on November 29. This aircraft had 80-inch-long leading edge slots in the wing, in order to test for performance improvements. Ship Two later broke its back in spectacular fashion during a heavy landing at Edwards Air Force Base while testing high sink rates. It was repaired with a stronger keel beam that became standard, and it went on to fly for United Airlines before it was retired in 1978.

As more DC-8s joined the test effort, it became apparent that high-speed drag, detected during the initial tests, was a serious problem. The problem was traced to interference between the wing and the engine pylon, which caused the JT3C-powered version to fly 20 knots slower than the guaranteed maximum cruise speed. The company

The big wing of the -62 boosted fuel capacity to more than 25,250 U.S. gallons. It also gave the aircraft a range of almost 7,400 nautical miles, making it an ideal candidate for eventual re-engining with CFM56 engines. This unusual DC-8-72, as the re-engined version was dubbed, began its life with United. It became the prototype Series 70 when it was acquired by Cammacorp. By the mid-1980s, it was operating as a corporate hack for the ARAMCO oil company.

Like United, Delta continued to use its "stretch-8s" well into the late 1980s, after conversion with CFM56 engines to meet tougher noise regulations. Delta's DC-8-71 "864" is pictured on finals at Miami in 1988 during its last few months in passenger service. The photo was taken more than 20 years after the aircraft was delivered to the airline as a Series 61. Later in 1988, it was converted to a freighter and began operation with United Parcel Service.

The reduced, 30-degree sweep and taller main gear allowed the DC-8 to be stretched much more easily than its main competitor, the Boeing 707. The result was the spectacularly stretched Series 60, which led to sales of an additional 262 aircraft. However, as attention switched to the wide-body DC-10, sales slowed to a trickle by the late 1960s. This aircraft, a DC-8-63CF now operated by Emery Worldwide Airlines, was one of the last to be delivered. It was handed over to the German charter airline Atlantis in 1971.

tested various wing modifications to improve range and payload, which were around 10 percent below projections. The wing leading edge slots, tried first on Ship Two, were extended and became standard. Starting with aircraft number 13, 3-foot-long, low-drag wingtip extensions were also added, increasing span to 142 feet, 5 inches. Another modification was a drooped flap, introduced to allow a 1.5-degree flap setting during cruise.

Although the aircraft was essentially underperforming, it was certificated in its initial configuration on August 31, 1959. The first two aircraft entered service within hours of each other on September 18, 1959. One flew for Delta, the other for United.

Further wing modifications followed in 1960. These developments were attempts to meet the original performance guarantees and included a sharper leading edge and lengthened leading edge slots. The modified section increased chord by 4 percent, thereby increasing wing area from 2,773 to 2,868 square feet. This provided more space for fuel. Tests proved spectacularly successful, with an 8 percent increase in range, a speed increase of 0.02 Mach, and up to 7,000 pounds of additional payload. The wing change was featured from aircraft number 148 forward, and Douglas offered to retrofit earlier aircraft.

Eventually, all early-model DC-8s were available with the wing. Beginning in February 1960, the designation system used to identify all models was changed in order to reflect the increasing variety of offerings. The initial domestic version with JT3C-6 turbojets, originally known as the DC-8A, was now called the Series 10. The follow-on DC-8As with the JT4A engines were known as the Series 20. The overwater DC-8Bs with JT4As were called Series 30s, and the Conway-powered DC-8s were designated Series 40. At the same time, DAC also revealed plans to use the upcoming JT3D turbofan engines on another version, dubbed the Series 50.

The more economical, fuel-efficient Series 50 quickly became a winner, outselling every other DC-8 version including the "Super DC-8" series that would soon follow. A total of 143 were delivered, almost three times the number of any other early model. It even outsold the most popular Super 60 series, the Series 63, by 36. The first Series 50 was the re-engined Series 10 prototype, which flew on December 20, 1960. The first production version was line number 120, delivered to KLM in April 1961.

Super Stretches

The surging growth in air travel throughout the first years of the 1960s prompted DAC to study the feasibility of stretching the basic DC-8. Thanks to a mixture of good fortune and planning, the aircraft was perfect for stretching because of its constant-dimension fuselage, its high (63-inch) ground clearance, and its relatively modest wing sweep angle. After devising what amounted to a simple

stretch of the Series 50, DAC designers hit upon the "Super 60" series, announced in April 1965.

The first member of the new family was the Series 61, which was stretched 20 feet ahead of the wing and 16 feet, 8 inches aft, creating the world's largest airliner. With an overall length of 187 feet, 5 inches, the aircraft retained its size dominance until the advent of the 747 at the end of the decade. The Series 61 retained the original wingspan of the Series 50. It could seat up to 269 people (as ruled by passenger emergency exit limits imposed by the FAA), although the standard, high-density arrangement chosen by most operators resulted in seating for 258. Firm orders for the Series 61 were placed by Eastern and United in April 1965. The first aircraft (line number 252) made its maiden flight on March 14, 1966. United received its first Series 61 on January 26, 1967.

Meanwhile, work was progressing on the next member of the new family, the Series 62. Largely a result of the long-range polar route requirements of

The DC-8's double-bubble fuselage cross section is clearly visible in this view of an Airborne Express freighter on finals. In the case of this unmodified Series 62, its Pratt & Whitney JT3D-7 turbofans are also visible. During tests the slim, extended pylons of the Series 62 caused wing flutter, or potentially destructive vibration. The problem was solved by redesigning the fuel system. This kept reserve fuel—and therefore weight—outboard in the wing for longer periods, thereby increasing stiffness.

A critical wing modification made early in the life of the DC-8 was the addition of leading edge slots to increase lift at low speed. The slots, which are clearly visible in this view, were covered by flush doors that automatically opened when the flaps were extended. The improvement allowed a takeoff weight increase of 8,000 pounds without any change in takeoff run.

SAS, the Series 62 incorporated a modified wing with increased span and area. The 148-foot, 5-inch span wing allowed a fuel capacity increase to 24,258 U.S. gallons. This refinement translated into increased range and payload. The range improvement was more significant, because the Series 62 fuselage stretch was relatively small compared to its larger sisters. Overall length was increased to only 157 feet, 3 inches with the addition of 3-foot, 3-inch plugs fore and aft of the wing.

The first two Series 62s were ordered by SAS on May 31, 1965. The first aircraft (line number 270) flew on August 29, 1966. Delivery was made to SAS the following May. In all, 67 Series 62s were built, of which 51 were completed as all-passenger versions. The -62s benefited from another series of aerodynamic changes to the engine pods and from repositioning of the pylons, which were extended 40 inches farther forward. These changes reduced the operating costs of the aircraft.

The third new version, the last DC-8 variant developed by DAC, was the Series 63. This aircraft

Power comes back as the wheels of this Aero Peru DC-8-62H reach for Miami's runway at the end of another flight from Lima. The passenger-carrying days of this aircraft, originally delivered to Alitalia as *Luigi Cherubini*, ended in 1994, when it began freight services with Airborne Express.

Faintly visible vortices spill over the wings of this Southern Air Transport-operated DC-8-73 as it makes an impressive departure from Los Angeles International in the gathering humidity of a fall evening. Compared with the Pratt & Whitney JT8D-209, which was offered as an alternative engine, the CFM56s reduced takeoff field length by as much as 850 feet.

The sheer elongation of the DC-8 stretch, which was extended with a 200-inch forward fuselage plug and a 240-inch plug aft, is clearly shown in this view of a Burlington Air Express DC-8-71F as it lines up for takeoff.

A Burlington Air Express DC-8-71F taxis after landing on a hot evening at Phoenix's Sky Harbor International Airport in Arizona. Note the chin-mounted air intakes for the air conditioning system and the limited ground clearance of the inboard engines. The switch to the CFM56 reduced fuel burn on a 3,000-nautical-mile trip by more than 21 percent and increased range by up to 800 nautical miles on the Series 61.

combined the bigger fuselage of the Series 61 with the bigger wing of the Series 62, producing a high-capacity aircraft with transatlantic range. As a result, the Series 63 was the most successful of the three versions. A total of 107 were delivered, including 41 all-passenger planes. The balance of the planes either combined passenger and freight capacities or were pure cargo craft. The first Series 63 took to the air on April 10, 1967. This aircraft was handed over to KLM in July of that year.

The Super Sixty program gave a vital boost to the DC-8. It prolonged production until May 1972, when Douglas delivered the 262nd Series 60, a Series 63, for SAS. Development of the DC-10 was well under way by then. The delivery

marked the end of the DC-8 line after 556 aircraft had been produced.

The Super Sixty also provided the foundation for one final chapter in the DC-8 story, the Series 70. The onset of new noise legislation and the availability of modern, higher-bypass-ratio turbofans, prompted DAC to look at re-engining the DC-8-60s in 1977. The company considered the Pratt & Whitney JT8D-209 engine, then being studied for the upcoming MD-80, and the CFM International CFM56.

With the deadline for a decision looming, United took action. The airline selected the CFM56 to serve as the replacement engine for 30 DC-8-60s, at a cost of $400 million. The new version was dubbed the Series 70 by DAC, which said the conversion would be managed by a new company called Cammacorp. Comprised of many ex-DAC employees and DC-8 workers, the El Segundo, California-based company organized a network involving DAC, CFM International, and Grumman Aerospace. Engines were shipped to Grumman's Long Island facility in New York for fitting with pods, cowls, and pylons. They were then shipped to the McDonnell Douglas plant in Tulsa, Oklahoma, where the retrofitting was performed.

The first re-engined aircraft, a Series 71, was returned to United in 1982. The 110th and last Series 70 delivery was made in April 1986. Of the 110 re-engined planes ordered in total, 44 were converted in Tulsa, 48 by Delta Airlines, and nine each by Air Canada and Unicon de Transports Aeriens (UTA) in France.

Thanks in part to the Series 70 program, the surviving population of DC-8s has remained much larger than the number of 707s. As of October 1998, about 280 DC-8s were in existence. Some, including even the older Series 50 aircraft, may operate well into the twenty-first century. Several companies, including Burbank Aeronautical Corporation in California, have developed Stage 3 hushkits for the older DC-8s. By late 1998, these companies were also flight-testing winglets to improve aerodynamic performance and boost range. Such developments indicate that the DC-8 is likely to be around in one form or another for many years to come.

A former Air Canada-owned DC-8-63, now operated by UPS as a re-engined -73, lifts off from Boeing Field in Seattle. UPS opted to prolong the life of its 49-member DC-8 fleet by upgrading the flight decks with electronic flight instrument systems. The upgrade also included an all-new Litton ring laser gyro inertial reference system. UPS plans to eventually replace its DC-8s with a fleet of Airbus A300-600Rs.

2

DC-9: TWINJET WORKHORSE

The remarkable DC-9 was America's first short-haul jet. It opened up a huge new market for Douglas and paved the way for three subsequent generations of twinjets—the last of which would outlive the company itself. Perhaps more than any other Douglas jetliner, the sturdy workhorse also firmly established the company's reputation for rugged construction and design.

The story of the DC-9 has several false starts. The first of them begins in 1947, when Douglas proposed a 28-seat design called the DC-9 as a replacement for its ubiquitous DC-3. The DC-9 name emerged again briefly in 1953, attached this time to a four-engine turboprop then being considered. The real story starts in 1956 when, at the request of Pan American, Douglas engineers began designing a smaller, short- to medium-range airliner that would complement the DC-8. The resulting DC-9, designated Model 2067, looked like a scaled-down DC-8 with four wing-mounted, underslung engines. Various Pratt & Whitney powerplants were considered, including the JT4A-5, the JT8A-2, and a promising "fan-jet" concept called the JTF10A-1.

As interest grew in short- to medium-haul jetliners of the DC-9 variety, so did the competition. By 1959 Sud Aviation, which pioneered the tail-mounted jet engine concept, had placed its Caravelle in service. The British company de Havilland was busy with the Trident; Boeing was working on a new trijet of its own, the 727. By early 1960, it became clear to DAC that its biggest American competitor was the 727, which had scooped major launch orders from United and Eastern by the end of the year. Boeing's early success quickly eliminated DAC's challenge. The 2067 project was shelved.

The effort nonetheless taught DAC some valuable lessons. The company's engineers had spent much of 1960 getting to know Sud Aviation and the Caravelle. The two companies signed a cooperative agreement in February 1960, under which DAC was to market the Caravelle in some areas outside of Europe. If the demand was sufficient, the agreement also contained a clause that would establish a Caravelle production line in Long Beach.

Because DAC's sales effort met with limited success in the United States, the agreement with the French company was soon terminated. However, the experience influenced a DAC design team. The team was attempting to develop a concept that would replace the myriad Convair and Martin piston airliners. At the time, these planes dominated those short-haul routes around the United States that had stage lengths of 500 miles or less. DAC outlined two baseline designs for a

By the mid-1990s, Northwest Airlines was the world's largest DC-9 operator, with more than 180 in service. The airline had invested in Airbus A320s, such as the one pictured taxiing in the background, for its larger needs. However, it considered the 717 (the former MD-95) a candidate for its DC-9 successor.

The vortilons visible beneath the leading edge and the adjacent wing fence were added to the DC-9 wing to prevent deep-stall incidents. Such incidents had affected the similar British BAC One-Eleven. The vortilon restricts spanwise air-flow and delays stall at angles of attack up to 30 degrees. This early aircraft, the sixth production example, was originally delivered to Air Canada in 1966. It is pictured here, 17 years later, as British Midland Airways' *Florentine Diamond*.

smaller jet. One proposal adopted a T-tail design with rear-mounted engines; the other offered a more conventional, underwing approach, resembling what would eventually become the 737.

Thanks to their knowledge of the Caravelle, the DAC engineers understood the inherent advantages of the tail-engined concept. These included a quiet cabin; a clean wing with good field performance and low drag; and favorable, one-engine-out handling characteristics. Other companies were working in a similar vein. In the United Kingdom, the British Aircraft Corporation was developing a T-tail design that would become the BAC One-Eleven. In the United States, Boeing was toying with a high tail for its new "Baby Boeing" jetliner project. The new enthusiasm for T-tails was not restricted to the West. Deep in the heart of Moscow, a Tupolev Design Bureau team led by Andrei Niholaevich Tupolev was busy sketching plans for the Soviet Union's first high tail jetliner, the Tu-134A.

Launching the DC-9

Because of the design benefits of the rear-engined configuration, the "compact jet" was adopted.

Reverse thrust, spoilers, brakes, and full flap bring this Kitty Hawk DC-9-15RC (Rapid Change) convertible freighter to a quick halt at Seatac International. The RC could be converted into a freighter in 75 minutes. In the all-freight configuration, it could carry a 25,000-pound payload over 1,100 miles. This particular aircraft was part of the launch order for RCs placed by Continental in 1965.

A brightly liveried Aero California DC-9-15 sets off from Los Angeles International for the resorts of Baja, Mexico. Production of these early Series 10 versions, which included the 14, 15, and 15RC/MC, continued until November 1968. A total of 137 aircraft were built.

DAC released details of the Model 2086 on April 11, 1962. The plan showed an aircraft capable of making short, multi-segment flights without refueling, yet offering performance similar to the bigger jets. At the request of American Airlines, DAC made further refinements to the design. The resulting Model 2086B was slightly larger, and was powered by a version of the new JT8D family, which American had chosen for its 727s. However, it was still below the 80,000-pound weight limit that DAC wanted to maintain in order to keep a two-crew cockpit.

To keep it simple, the 2086B was envisioned as a direct evolution from the airframe design, structural concepts, and systems know-how of the DC-8. The newer concept featured a much shorter version of the DC-8's double-bubble fuselage, supported by an elegantly simple wing. It

Svipdag Viking scurries past a clutch of Aeroflot Tupolev Tu-154s at Leningrad (now St. Petersburg) Pulkovo airport. Only 10 Series 20s (designated DC-9-21s) were built, in order to meet a special order from SAS. The "Sport" DC-9, as SAS crews sometimes called the aircraft for its impressive performance, combined the short fuselage of the Series 10 with the improved wing and more powerful engines of the large Series 30.

The high lift wing of the Series 30 featured full-span leading edge slats and double-slotted flaps, all of which can be seen clearly in this photograph of an Eastern DC-9-31 just about to land. Together with a 4-foot span increase at the tips, the new wing enabled DAC to gradually increase the takeoff weight of the Series 30 from 98,000 pounds to 121,000 pounds. This particular aircraft remained in operation for Northwest more than 30 years after its initial delivery to Eastern.

was designed to provide economical, high-speed operation for short ranges, as well as excellent low-speed characteristics. The aircraft had good longitudinal stability, thanks to careful compromises between wing sweep, airfoil design, horizontal tail location, tail airfoil design, and elevator control system. It also incorporated excellent high mach number maneuvering characteristics with comfortable control forces, a high buffet boundary, and none of the pitch-up tendencies that had plagued earlier swept wing designs.

To ensure wide operational flexibility, the 2086B had a center of gravity range up to 25 percent of the mean aerodynamic chord. It was also designed with a large rudder and lateral control spoilers that

Aviaco's *Juan Sebastian Elcano,* a DC-9-32, rests between European charter flights on a warm evening in Palma, Majorca. The attractive economics of the DC-9 soon made it a popular option with inclusive tour operators as the charter market boomed in Europe during the 1970s.

After surviving the bankruptcy of both Eastern and Midway, this DC-9-31 found new life in the Caribbean with Air Aruba. By the mid-1990s, the airline had graduated to operating MD-88s and in 1998 took delivery of its first MD-90s.

ensured good handling characteristics in crosswinds up to 30 knots. The wing was carefully designed to give high lift and good stall behavior with significant camber, large leading edge radii, and trailing edge flaps rather than leading edge devices.

The wing also featured "vortilons," small chordwise fences on the lower wing surface that improved control at high angles of attack up to 30 degrees. In most attitudes, the vortilons were aft of the area where the airflow "stagnated," so they had little effect. However, when the aircraft was in a potentially dangerous, nose-up attitude, the vortilons poked past the stagnation point and triggered vortices. The vortices extended over the upper wing surface and limited the spanwise flow, thereby preserving lift on the outboard wing sections, so the inner wing would stall first. In a swept wing design, this makes the nose pitch sharply down, enabling the crew to recover control quickly. The vortilons also reduced the downwash from the wing on the tail, which helped crews recover from potential deep stalls.

Deep stalls were a problem for T-tail designs. At angles greater than 30 degrees, aircraft with T-tails can lock into a stall because the horizontal tail is partially blanketed in the turbulent downwash from the wings. Lessons learned from the crash of a BAC One-Eleven under such circumstances resulted in a larger tail for the DC-9. The horizontal tail span was increased from 30.7 feet in the original design to 36.85 feet. Chord was also increased, and the total area was boosted by 23.1 percent to 275.5

square feet. Elevator power, ordinarily derived from aerodynamic servotabs, was augmented with a supplementary power unit. This unit drove the elevators downward when the tabs were deflected down by more than 19 degrees. A "stick-shaker" was also fitted. The device literally rattled the control column, warning the crew when the aircraft was approaching a stall condition.

While the design came together, many at DAC were worried that the rest of the company was beginning to fall apart. An important $300 million military contract, the Douglas Skybolt, was canceled in late 1962. Although there were still plenty of DC-8 orders on hand, the company faced a financial crisis. Unable to internally raise the additional $100 million needed for the new twinjet project, and unwilling to merge with its keen suitor McDonnell Aircraft, the company devised a unique risk-sharing agreement with companies in 27 states and Canada. The move included a deal with de Havilland Aircraft of Canada, under which DAC could use an old Avro factory at Malton to make the wings and parts of the empennage. This ultimately led to the establishment of McDonnell Douglas Canada, which would build virtually all subsequent DAC jetliner wings.

Satisfied with its network of new partners and gambling heavily on the prospect of imminent orders, DAC gave the go-ahead on April 8, 1963, for what was now officially the DC-9. John Brizendine, the DC-8 program manager, was appointed by Donald Douglas, Sr., to head the crucial new program. The first order from Delta, for 15 firm with 15 options, was announced on April 25. Later that year, DAC received an order for three planes from Bonanza, which had originally selected the BAC One-Eleven, and an order for six from Air Canada. All orders were for the initial production version which, like the DC-8 before it, was dubbed the -10.

Construction of parts began in July 1963, and final assembly at Long Beach commenced the following March. Douglas rolled out the first aircraft on January 12, 1965. The second, destined for Delta, emerged right behind it. The first flight

took place on February 25, crewed by chief engineering pilot George Jansen, copilot Paul Pattern, and flight test engineer Duncan Walker. It lasted 2 hours, 13 minutes, ending with a landing at Edwards Air Force Base in California's high desert. The flawless flight set the standard for a trouble-free test program that concluded with type certification on November 23, 1965. The five test aircraft in the program accumulated 1,280 flight hours and conducted more than 2,000 stalls, during which the DC-9s recovered from angles of attack up to 31.5 degrees.

The first revenue service by a DC-9-10 took place six days later, when Delta substituted it for other equipment on an Atlanta-to-Memphis route. However, the new twinjet officially entered passenger service on the airline's routes from Atlanta in December 1965.

Growing Family

The ultimate success of the DC-9 and the MD-80 that followed it was based on the basic flexibility of the design and the seemingly infinite number of versions that could be derived from the original baseline model. This process was fueled by competition between airlines such as Eastern, United, and Lufthansa, all of which wanted something bigger than the DC-9-10.

DAC outlined an "advanced" DC-9 with a 9-foot, 6-inch stretch. This was later extended by another 5 feet, 5 inches. The new version was successively designated the DC-9-151, the DC-9B, and the DC-9-20. It had a bigger wing with an extended 2-foot tip on either side, giving it a span of 93.3 feet. To maintain good takeoff performance at the higher weights envisaged, full span slats were added to the leading edge, and a double-slotted flap design was added to the trailing edge.

By the time Eastern Airlines placed a launch order for 24 of the "advanced" versions in February 1965, the benefits of the bigger wing combined with

The double-bubble fuselage cross-sectional concept worked very successfully on the DC-8. It was also put to good use on the DC-9, as can be seen in this evening view of the SAS DC-9-41 *Bent Viking*. The DC-9-41 was a 6-foot, 2-inch stretch of the DC-9-30. It was produced to meet the high density, short-range requirements of SAS routes. Note the foreign object damage (FOD) deflector around the nose gear wheels.

the original -10 fuselage had begun to attract interest from SAS. The larger stretch was subsequently re-designated the Series 30. The re-winged variant for SAS, which featured the shorter fuselage, became the Series 20. The Series 30 would become the most popular member of the DC-9 family, accounting for 662 of the 976 aircraft built. Ultimately, only 10 of the Series 20 were built, but the "Sport" version (as it was nicknamed by SAS crews) remained popular with the airline due to its sprightly performance.

The first Series 30 (line number 48) flew on August 1, 1966, and was delivered to Eastern on February 27 of the following year. The first Series 20 (line number 382) flew on September 18, 1968, and entered service with SAS on January 27, 1969. Final Series 20 delivery was made to SAS the following May.

SAS was also instrumental in the launch of the next major version, the Series 40. In response to the airline's need for a high-density, short-range aircraft, DAC stretched the fuselage by another 6

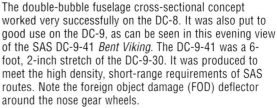

Netherlands flag carrier KLM (Koninklyke Luchtvaart Maatschappy) continued its long tradition of operating Douglas products with the DC-9-33RC, pictured nosing up to stand at London's Heathrow. Note the freight door, which led to its later career in the United States with Airborne Express and Evergreen International. KLM operated every Douglas commercial type from the DC-2 to the MD-11, including the little-known DC-5. KLM bought a third of the total DC-5 production run of 12.

Before the transition to the MD-80, the ultimate DC-9 model was the Series 50. Developed to meet a Swissair requirement, the DC-9-51 was the longest Douglas twin at the time, extending 133 feet, 6 inches. Note the nose-mounted strake on this Finnair example. The strake was added to improve pitch stability after the 8-foot fuselage stretch.

feet, 2 inches, giving it an overall length of 125 feet, 7 inches. The company made more-powerful JT8D-9, -11, or -15 engines available with the Series 40s, while increasing maximum seating to 132. SAS launched the line in February 1966 with an order for 10, and the first flight of a Series 40 (line number 218) took place on November 28, 1967. Despite a heavy marketing campaign, only SAS and Toa Domestic of Japan ordered the aircraft. A total of 71 Series 40s had been built when production ended in 1979.

The late 1960s also saw some new business in the form of military versions called the C-9. All were based on the DC-9-30 and were known as the C-9A Nightingale to the U.S. Air Force, which used them for aeromedical evacuation. The U.S. Navy and the Marine Corps called these aircraft the C-9B Skytrain II, using a number of them as logistic transports.

The real commercial emphasis, however, remained on extending the DC-9 family and finding new business. This business materialized in the early 1970s after discussions with Swissair, which was looking for a larger-capacity aircraft to complement its DC-9-30s. The Series 50, the fifth and last major DC-9 variant, was officially launched in July 1973, when Swissair ordered 10. The first aircraft (line number 757) flew on December 17, 1974, and was delivered the following August.

The Series 50 was stretched 8 feet farther than the Series 40, giving it an overall length of 133 feet, 6 inches. The length was such that a small strake was fixed to each side of the forward fuselage in order to restore full longitudinal stability.

SAS DC-9-41s and an Iberia DC-9-33RC provide evidence of the DC-9s pan-European popularity as a British Airways Concorde is towed past Heathrow's Terminal Two. Other major DC-9 carriers on the continent included Alitalia, Austrian, Finnair, KLM, and Swissair, all of which subsequently switched to Airbus and Boeing.

Powered by 15,000-pound-thrust JT8D-15 engines or 16,000-pound-thrust JT8D-17s, the Series 50 could carry up to 139 passengers in a high-density layout and had a range of 2,110 nautical miles with maximum fuel. To cope with the increased gross weight of 121,000 pounds, which was almost double that of the original Series 10, the aircraft also featured an improved anti-skid braking system. Due to effects of the longer fuselage, the angle of the thrust reversers was moved around by 17 degrees from the vertical to prevent any reingestion of hot gas.

The Series 50 development proved significant to the order book. A total of 96 were built before the final delivery took place in April 1981. The project also proved that the basic T-tail concept was still viable with longer stretches, and that, given the available engine power, the aircraft could be extended even farther. With an eye to additional growth, DAC began studying new variants, which would ultimately form the record-breaking MD-80 family. The company produced DC-9s from 1965 to 1982, building a total of 976. The very last DC-9 (line number 1084) was a Series 32 for the U.S. Navy that was handed over on October 28, 1982. The first age of the Douglas twinjet was over. However, another had already begun.

3

DC-10: ENTER THE TRIJET

Thanks to its unusual tail-mounted engine and its blunt nose, the DC-10 has been a distinctive sight at airports around the world for almost 30 years. It was to prove the best-selling wide-body trijet ever built, and it provided the foundation for the MD-11. As with many generations of Douglas designs before it, the strength and flexibility of the DC-10 also meant that many would enjoy second lives as freighters well into the twenty-first century.

The story of the DC-10 goes back to the days of the Cold War, a period of tension between the superpowers that began in the 1950s. The tension forced the U.S. Air Force to re-examine its military airlift requirements. In 1962, it established Project Forecast to review all the emerging technology that might be useful. The field of jet engine development spurred particular excitement. At the time, General Electric was studying huge new, high-bypass-ratio engines, which were called turbofans. These engines offered much higher power-to-weight ratios, higher thrust growth potential, and fuel consumption savings of up to 20 percent. The prospect of the new engines convinced the USAF to search for an enormous new strategic transport that could carry as many as 700 troops directly to a battle area.

Known as the CX-HLS (Experimental Cargo/Heavy Logistics System), the program sparked fierce competition between Boeing, Douglas, and Lockheed. All three came up with concepts for vast aircraft, but Lockheed was awarded the contract and went on to build the C-5 Galaxy. Despite losing the competition, both Boeing and Douglas realized that their intensive design efforts could be applied to a new civil transport, much larger than either the 707s or the DC-8s that ruled the airways at the time.

Boeing completely realigned its big jet effort, concentrating on a low-wing, wide-body design that could be quickly adapted into a freighter when the inevitable wave of supersonic airliners took over the main passenger trunk routes. In April 1966, Boeing launched the 747 with an order for 25 from Pan American.

Meanwhile, Douglas was prepared to be even more ambitious. It sketched out plans for a massive, 650-passenger, four-engine jet based on design principles and power plant options the company had studied for its CX-HLS proposal. The airlines were interested, particularly in the behemoth's ludicrously low seat-mile costs, but they worried that it was simply too large. The travel boom of the 1960s was well under way at the time. Traffic was expanding at the phenomenal rate of about 15 percent every year, but even this level of growth did not convince the larger airlines to gamble on the design that Douglas called the DC-10. But Douglas was determined to play a part in the emerging wide-body era. The company continued to study twin, trijet, and four jet DC-10 designs.

The chance to enter the market with the right product finally came in 1966, when a loyal customer issued a specification for an "airbus."

A veteran United DC-10-10 trundles in to land in perfect weather at Los Angeles International. In more inclement weather the DC-10 was certified to land in 90-degree crosswinds up to 30 knots.

With thrust reversers deployed and everything "hanging out," an American Airlines DC-10-10 slows after landing at Los Angeles International. American had more to do with Douglas's first wide-body than any other carrier. By issuing a requirement for an "air bus" in April 1966, it sowed the seeds for the DC-10 and the Lockheed Tristar. It also placed the first order for the DC-10 in February 1968.

American Airlines had also recognized the potential of the new generation of turbofans, and its specification included a requirement that would have been impossible with the older engines. The airbus specification called for a large-capacity, medium-range aircraft that could carry a full load of 250 passengers plus 5,000 pounds of freight from Chicago to Los Angeles. The aircraft, which American envisioned as a twinjet, would also have good enough field performance to fly to Chicago with a full payload out of the short, 5,000-foot runway at New York's La Guardia Airport on a 90-degree-Fahrenheit day.

The American Airlines requirement set off a chain reaction between Douglas, Lockheed, and the other major airlines in the United States. Both of the manufacturers responded with similar twin-engine designs seating up to 300. However, when more airlines were canvassed, it quickly became apparent that a trijet design was preferable. There were several reasons behind this conclusion. First, more airlines were interested in an aircraft with coast-to-coast range. Because fan engines were still in their infancy, this was considered commercially feasible only with three jets. Second, a range of operational issues nudged the companies toward trijets. These included less acceptable weather limits for takeoff and landing, the impossibility of ferrying the aircraft on only one engine and more severe hot and high performance limitations. Third, the airlines were nervous at the prospect of operating a large-capacity twinjet over water. Both Douglas and Lockheed were told that trijets were a must for longer-range versions.

At the time, there were greater uncertainties threatening the future of the embryonic DC-10, and the future of Douglas in general. The company's financial strength had gradually waned since the end of the 1950s. During the ensuing period, DAC experienced a steep reduction in military work due to its lack of success in USAF competitions. In addition, the prolonged development of the DC-8 caused problems that culminated in 1966 with a serious cash flow crisis. By October 1966, Douglas needed some $400 million to meet its commitments.

Evening sunlight bathes the polished fuselage and smooth skin of an American Airlines DC-10-10 as it nears touchdown. Note the full-span leading edge slats and double-slotted trailing edge flaps that give the aircraft good field performance. The 35-degree sweep of the 155-foot, 4-inch span wing is also illustrated in this view.

Pratt & Whitney JT9D engines differentiate this DC-10 as a Series 40. The model was originally developed as the DC-10-20, but Northwest—the sole customer at the time—talked the manufacturer into calling it the Series 40. Like the DC-10-30, it featured the increased 165-foot, 4-inch span wing and center main landing gear.

Although the DC-8 and DC-9 order books were bulging, the cash crisis threatened the entire company. Lazard Freres, a Wall Street company specializing in financial analysis, was called in. By December 1966, the analysts told Douglas that it had virtually no option but to seek a merger. Various suitors came and went, including North American Aviation, General Dynamics, Fairchild, and Garret Industries. Finally, on January 13, 1967, Douglas officials accepted an offer from the McDonnell Corporation, which agreed to invest $68.7 million in the company. On April 28, 1967, the Douglas Aircraft Company was taken over. It became the Douglas Aircraft Company division of McDonnell Douglas (MDC).

The move bolstered DAC's design strength and allowed DC-10 development to continue with renewed vigor. By the fall of 1967, the twin had been firmly rejected and the DC-10 trijet design was falling into place. Intense negotiations with American Airlines were rewarded with a contract for 25 planes, received on February 19, 1968. The American Airlines order called for 25 aircraft on a firm basis and optioned 25 more. It covered the initial domestic version, which was dubbed the DC-10-10. Although this was the first order for any big trijets, MDC board members were unsure whether they should commit to the program without additional orders. Meanwhile the competing Lockheed trijet, named the L-1011 TriStar, stole the spotlight from the DC-10 by becoming officially launched on April 1, 1968. It was launched with commitments for up to 144 planes from Eastern, TWA, and a financial group called Air Holdings.

Japan Air Lines was the only other customer for the DC-10-40. As shown in this view, taken on the ramp at Tokyo's Haneda airport, the versions used for domestic services differed in that they did not have the center main gear. Note the bulged number two (tail) engine intake, denoting the higher mass flow requirements of the P&W-powered aircraft.

With the TriStar's lead threatening to expand, it was a huge relief to the DAC workforce when United signed for 30 DC-10-10s plus another 30 options on April 25. The order was big enough to satisfy the MDC board, and the DC-10 was launched.

Trijet Design

Despite its huge size, the basic structural design of the DC-10 followed the blueprint of the DC-8 and DC-9. As a result, there was little use of titanium, steel, honeycomb, glass fiber, or a manufacturing technique known as bonding, or any other materials or methods that were relatively unusual at the time. Nor were skin milling or integral stringers involved. Instead, the fuselage was a classic structure of closely spaced frames and stringers with small, thin skin panels. The biggest panel was 400 inches by 90 inches. Skins were butt-jointed with internal and external doublers for extra strength. Titanium was used for "tear stoppers."

The individual wing halves were attached through multi-bolt joints between the wing and fuselage skins, and by long spar caps that tied the front and rear box-spar booms to the center section. The wing skins, which came in the shape of three huge planks for the top and four for the lower surface, were machine-tapered with riveted stringers.

In general, the structure was therefore based on the same fail-safe and fatigue-resistant design principles that had established the company's reputation for producing tremendously rugged airframes. The DC-10 was originally expected to have an economic service life of 20 years and a

United's massive 1968 order for up to 60 DC-10s ensured the launch of the wide-body and a long association with the trijet. Here a trijet is shown touching down at Seatac 30 years later. By this time, the DC-10-10 was in the twilight of its passenger-carrying career with United. The bulk of these aircraft were destined for conversion into freighters for Federal Express.

minimum fatigue life of 120,000 flight hours. The domestic version was designed for up to 84,000 cycles. A cycle is a complete flight, including take-off and landing. The intercontinental version, dubbed the DC-10-30, was designed for 60,000 cycles. By late 1998, the DC-10 with the greatest amount of service time was an ex-Swissair DC-10-30 then in service with Northwest. The aircraft had amassed more than 25,300 cycles. The highest-cycle aircraft was a former Japan Air Lines DC-10-40 flying as a freighter, which had built up more than 40,650 cycles.

On the outside, the DC-10 was distinguished by its relatively sharply swept wings supporting an engine beneath each, and by an unusual, tail-mounted center engine position. The manufacturers argued the merits of DAC's "straight-through" engine inlet and duct versus Lockheed's faired-in tail engine and S-duct, which were arguably more pleasing from an aesthetic point of view. There were good points about both solutions, but DAC adamantly insisted that its design was the best. The differences were pronounced. The DC-10's engine was mounted in the tail fin itself and hung on a strut that was cantilevered aft of the fin spar. The inlet was supported by a large, banjo-shaped fitting that allowed air to enter the engine head-on. The

TriStar, on the other hand, enclosed the center engine at the very back of the fuselage, at the base of the fin. Air was ducted into it via an S-shaped duct. The low-mounted centerline thrust of the L-1011 engine allowed Lockheed to place the other engines farther out on the wing. This meant that the TriStar wings were slightly lighter in construction, because they benefited from greater bending relief.

Former Douglas engineering vice president Dale Warren recalled that the DC-10 design team looked at five different design concepts, including an S-duct. "In the end, we ended up with a straight-through duct, which required the use of enormous forgings to span the duct. These forgings weighed around 5,000 pounds before being milled, and when they came out of the workshop they weighed about 500 pounds by the end. They were the largest forgings in the world at the time, and we patented them."

Despite DAC's overt confidence in its tail design, potential drag problems caused a great deal of concern. The engineers need not have worried, as 14,000 hours of wind tunnel tests, many of them focused on the tail configuration, revealed very little in the way of drag effects. In fact, most of the measured drag was attributed to skin friction rather than the shape of the tail itself.

An Iberia DC-10-30 taxis in toward the airline's Miami hub after a flight from Madrid, Spain. The center gear, seen clearly here, was needed to support the extra weight of a center section fuel tank. The Series 30 could carry as much as 38,150 U.S. gallons of useable fuel, compared to 26,570 U.S. gallons in the Series 10.

The wing was of conventional design. It was swept at 35 degrees at the quarter chord position, which is one-quarter of the way back along a line drawn from the leading edge to the trailing edge. It had a sharp leading edge consisting of forward-moving leading edge slats that only marginally deflected down, thereby increasing wing area without adding much drag. Wing area was 3,861 square feet on the 155-foot, 4-inch span -10 wing and 3,921 square feet on the slightly larger -30 wing. The -30 wing was extended with longer tips, producing a span of 165 feet, 4 inches. The -30 wing was fitted with two sections of trailing edge flaps. On landing, the trailing edge flap and slat separated to form a double slot, while the leading edge

slat extended farther to make an effective slot. Over the inboard flap section, the lower shroud deflected upward to improve the slot shape where the wing was thickest.

Another difference between the -10 and the -30, and the only visible way of telling them apart, was an extra two-wheel main undercarriage unit on the heavier aircraft. The unit was located under the wing center section. It was fitted to counter the extra weight of the fuel carried in the center section of the longer-range version. The extra wheels, together with the two standard four-wheel main gear units and the two-wheel nose gear, produced pavement loadings on a par with the 707 and only slightly lower than fully loaded DC-8-63s.

Into Service

The first DC-10 built at Long Beach took to the air on August 29, 1970, some five weeks after the model rolled out. Commanded by chief project pilot Clifford Stout, Douglas' first wide-body took off at a weight of 340,000 pounds—70,000 pounds below its maximum takeoff weight—after a ground roll of 4,980 feet. During the 3-hour, 26-minute flight, the four-man crew took N10DC through basic handling evaluations, then landed at Edwards Air Force Base.

By this time, DAC had received orders for 119, with options on an additional 122. Of these, 75 were for the DC-10-10 version, while 30 were for the -30. The balance consisted of 14 orders for another version, dubbed the DC-10-20. Unlike all the other versions, which were powered by variants of the General Electric CF6, the -20 was powered by the Pratt & Whitney JT9D—the same engine that powered all versions of the 747 for the first seven years of production. However, Pratt & Whitney did not achieve a similar monopoly on the DC-10. Ultimately, 42 P&W-powered versions were sold to two customers, Northwest and JAL. Following pressure from Northwest (who wanted to appear more progressive), the DC-10-20 was also renamed the DC-10-40. The -40 became the second version of the DC-10 to fly when the first

The DC-10-30's range of up to 5,650 nautical miles with 277 passengers and baggage made it the ideal aircraft for long, medium/thin routes. Union de Transports Aeriens (UTA) used the aircraft on routes of this type to destinations in French colonial Africa. This aircraft, dating from 1973, was tragically destroyed in midair by a terrorist bomb. It crashed in the Massif de Termit region of Niger in September 1989, just weeks after this photograph was taken.

DC-10-30s spread far and wide in service. This aircraft, originally delivered to Air New Zealand in October 1975, passed into the hands of Linhas Aereas de Mocambique for several years. It then entered into service with AOM French Airlines.

model took to the air as a Series 20 on February 28, 1972. It was certificated on October 20 of that year and entered service with Northwest on December 13, 1972. Northwest bought 22 of the planes, while JAL purchased 20.

Certification of the original DC-10-10 version had been obtained on July 29, 1971, after a 1,551-hour test program that lasted 11 months and involved five aircraft. The first -10 entered service with American Airlines, flying between Los Angeles and Chicago on August 5, 1971—just five years and four months after the airline had issued the original specification. The five biggest "trunk" airlines in the United States purchased 113 of the -10s built, or 90 percent of the total. Between them, American and

United took 76 aircraft, or 60 percent of the type's total sales. A subvariant, the convertible freighter known as the DC-10-10CF, sold exclusively to U.S. airlines. However, only nine were built.

In terms of both performance and sales, the most successful version was the longer-range DC-10-30. Douglas planned its intercontinental version from the start, offering the aircraft with the higher-thrust (45,600 pounds) GE CF6-10 engine, later identified as the CF6-50. Although the GE-powered alternative was launched later than the virtually identical P&W-powered DC-10-20, it was far more successful in the long run. This was probably due in large part to the fact that problems had been experienced with the JT9D engine on 747s.

An Ecuatoriana DC-10-30 adds a splash of color to the typically busy scene at Los Angeles International. The aircraft was handed over to Swissair in November 1972, becoming one of the first Series 30s ever delivered. It passed into Ecuatoriana service 11 years later and, except for periods in storage, served the airline continuously into the late 1990s. Note the military code on the tail, denoting its unusual dual identity.

Engine-related issues also severely affected the pace at which the TriStar was developed. The aircraft was virtually wedded to the Rolls-Royce RB.211 engine. Problems with engine development forced the British manufacturer into bankruptcy in 1971, while cost overruns of $2 billion on Lockheed's C-5 program added to the hurdles facing the TriStar team. The result was an extended delay to the proposed long-range L-1011-8, which would have competed head-on with the DC-10-20/30. After Rolls-Royce was rescued by the British government and problems with the Galaxy contract had been overcome, Lockheed began working on a "hot and high" -200 version. However, the TriStar was not able to compete with the DC-10-30 until the -500 long-range variant was launched in August 1976. By then it was too late. The company optimistically forecast sales of up to 200 of the -500s, but when production ended in 1983, only 50 had been sold. The end of production also marked the end of trijet competition.

The DC-10-30/40 differed from earlier DC-10 models mainly in that it had a large auxiliary tank in the center wing body. The tank held up to 98,000 pounds of fuel, boosting total capacity to 245,570 pounds. Together with the additional lift of the larger span wing, this gave the DC-10-30 a range of 5,650 nautical miles when carrying a typical load of 277 passengers. The -40, which used the slightly less powerful JT9Ds, could normally fly a distance of 5,550 nautical miles with the same load. Some -30s were also delivered as -30ERs, or extended range models. These planes were fitted with an additional fuel tank containing up to 3,200 gallons in the rear cargo hold. Equipped with either this tank or a smaller, 1,530-gallon tank, the -30ERs had a maximum range of 5,800 to 6,150 nautical miles with 277 passengers.

The DC-10-30 was formally launched on June 7, 1969, when a group called KSSU placed orders for 36 aircraft. The group was comprised of airlines that were loyal DC operators, including KLM, SAS, Swissair, and UTA. These customers regarded the DC-10-30 as a logical successor to their much-traveled DC-8s. The -30 development aircraft (line number 46) rolled out of Building 84 on June 1, 1972, and flew 20 days later. The minimum-change philosophy adopted for the long-range version worked, and DAC was awarded

One of the last commercial DC-10-30s made, this Japan Air System aircraft was delivered in 1988. Note the Peter Pan promotional cartoon figures on the side and the colorful livery, which JAS adapted from the original scheme used by Airbus Industrie for its demonstrator A300.

FAA type certification just five months later, on November 21, 1972. Swissair became the first to operate the DC-10-30 when the airline began using it for transatlantic service on December 15, only two days after the first -40 entered service.

Production of the DC-10 Series continued for 18 years. The last phase of production was boosted by a USAF order for 60 KC-10A Extender tankers. This variant was basically a -30CF (Convertible Freighter) with modifications for aerial refueling and other changes. The first of the KC-10As was delivered to the USAF on March 17, 1981. Including these aircraft, total production of the Series 30 reached 266. Excluding the KC-10As, roughly 50 percent of all deliveries took place in the first four full years of production. Eighty-five percent of all deliveries had been completed by the end of 1980.

Another DC-10 version was belatedly developed for the Mexican airlines Aeromexico and Mexicana. Dubbed the Series 15, the first "hot and high" version was delivered in June 1981. A total of seven were built, and the last one was delivered in 1983. Except for its engine, the -15 was identical to the high-gross-weight, 455,000-pound DC-10-10. It was powered by CF6-50C2F engines, rated at 46,500-pound thrust, instead of the standard, 41,000-pound-thrust CF6-6D/6D1s. The Series -15 aircraft could carry 275 passengers and a full fuel load for 3,750 nautical miles after taking off from an 11,000-foot runway at 8,000 feet above mean sea level.

Despite special versions like the -15 and the KC-10A, sales of the DC-10 began to dry up in the late 1980s. Part of the cause was the planned production of the MD-11 (see chapter 5), but increased competition from long-distance, high-capacity twins produced by Boeing and Airbus was a more important factor. DC-10 production finally ceased in 1989, when the 266th -30 was delivered to Nigeria Airways. It was the 446th and last DC-10/KC-10 to be built.

Accidents and Lessons

Tragically, the DC-10 became well known to the public because of a number of serious accidents that occurred in the 1970s and 1980s. All of the disasters led to design improvements and safety enhancements—not only in DC-10s, but throughout the entire fleet of wide-bodied jetliners.

The sheer ruggedness of the DC-10, a typically strong Douglas design, is exemplified by the story behind this Series 30. The aircraft was originally delivered to Ariana Afghan Airlines in 1979. In September 1984, the DC-10 was approaching Khwaya Ranuash airport in Kabul with 321 aboard. It was hit in midair by what is thought to have been a ground-to-air missile. Despite crippling damage to the hydraulics, the wing, and the port engine, which essentially detached from the aircraft, the DC-10 somehow landed safely. It was later repaired and entered service with British Caledonian as G-MULL before subsequently becoming part of the British Airways fleet.

As the DC-10 fleet flies into the twenty-first century, the most important new development is the MD-10 program from Boeing and Federal Express. Up to 120 aircraft, including this former United DC-10-10CF already in FedEx service, are being radically updated. They will receive a two-crew cockpit based on the MD-11 configuration. At least 60 former American and United DC-10s are also being converted to freighters for Federal Express as part of the program.

The first major accident involved a Turkish Airlines -30 that crashed into a forest near Paris in March 1974, killing all aboard. The aircraft was climbing through 12,000 feet en route to London when a small rear bulk cargo door on the port aft side blew open. This caused instant depressurization of the lower aft section of the hold, which in turn resulted in the structural failure of the cabin floor. The floor collapsed downward under the sudden pressure change, severing the control cables that ran through the floor to the tail. The aircraft went into a shallow dive, striking the forest at a speed of 420 knots just 77 seconds after the depressurization.

DAC had modified the door and its locking mechanism after a rear cargo door separated from an American Airlines DC-10 over Windsor, Ontario, in June 1972. However, not all the modifications were incorporated quickly enough into the fleet. This resulted in another decompression incident involving a National Airlines DC-10 over Albuquerque, New Mexico, in 1973, as well as the Paris crash of 1974. The incidents taught all manufacturers and airlines the vital importance of responding quickly and thoroughly to recommended safety modifications. It also resulted in widespread adoption of through-floor venting in all wide-body designs. With the new venting system, pressure would equalize quickly in the event of sudden decompression.

Unfortunately, the DC-10 was back in the news five years later, when an American Airlines DC-10-10 crashed shortly after takeoff on May 25, 1979. The plane was departing from Chicago's O'Hare, and the crash killed all 271 on board. It resulted from the separation of a wing-mounted engine after takeoff. The engine rotated back over the wing. The crew might have been able to save the plane were it not for damage caused to the hydraulic system and high lift devices as the engine broke free. The subsequent investigation concluded that the cause was not a design flaw. Instead, an engine had been incorrectly lifted onto the strut after maintenance. However, the FAA reacted while memories of Paris were still fresh in the minds of the media. The agency withdrew the type certificate on June 6. Some observers felt the withdrawal was an overreaction.

In any case, all DC-10s were grounded for more than a month. This caused a great deal of

A Mexican-Argentinian-operated STAF DC-10-30CF cargo-passenger convertible freighter sits in the January sunshine at Miami in 1998. Note the large, 102-inch by 140-inch main deck side cargo door near the nose. A total of 28 Series 30CFs, 9 Series 30AFs (all freight), and 60 KC-10A military cargo/tankers were built on the line.

chaos, particularly in the United States. The restriction was lifted on July 13, but, thanks to bad publicity and media hype, the DC-10's reputation suffered in the minds of the traveling public for some time. In response, American Airlines began calling its fleet "Luxury Liners" instead of "DC-10 Luxury Liners." However, a study conducted in 1983 by the Massachusetts Institute of Technology revealed that there was no discernible public avoidance of the aircraft within six to nine months after the accident. Passenger levels had returned to pre-accident levels.

Another crash investigation did refer to the DC-10's design in assigning responsibility. This crash involved the loss of a United Airlines DC-10-10 at Sioux City, Iowa, on July 19, 1989. The accident resulted from loss of control following the uncontained failure of the number two (center) engine. The engine's fan disk broke, scattering debris through the empennage and rupturing all three of the DC-10's hydraulic systems at a critical spot. The hydraulic power controlling all the flight control surfaces quickly faded. The crew cleverly

attempted to maneuver the crippled DC-10 in for a landing by using engine power alone to control the aircraft. Thanks to the crew's valiant efforts, the aircraft made it to the airport at Sioux City. However, control was lost just before touchdown, which resulted in a bad crash landing. Miraculously, 184 of the 296 people on board survived.

The National Transportation Safety Board ruled that United and GE shared responsibility, because the accident stemmed from the failure of the CF6-6 fan disk. Investigation revealed that the disk had contained an undetected crack. Although the DC-10 itself was not blamed, the board said the hydraulic systems on the DC-10 were not protected against such a catastrophic failure.

In response to the accident, NASA joined with McDonnell Douglas, Pratt & Whitney, and Honeywell to develop a system called Propulsion Controlled Aircraft (PCA). The system takes advantage of the precise engine control made possible by today's full-authority digital engine control (FADEC) units. In essence, the system replicates what the United crew did manually. The PCA computer

The capacity of the DC-10 made it ideal for large-scale, inclusive tour and charter operations. Typical two-class-scheduled airline layouts provided seating for 255 in economy and 22 in business or first, whereas all-economy charter layouts could exceed 300. The German operator Condor flew its DC-10s in the highest-known seat density layout of 370. Here a Balair DC-10-30 noses into Zurich with a load of 264 economy and 63 "club-class" passengers.

simply interprets the commands of the pilot and, instead of routing them to flight control surfaces, sends them to the FADECs. If the pilot wants to turn right, for example, power is increased to the left engine. If he wants to climb, power on both engines is increased, and vice versa for descent. A fully working PCA system was demonstrated on an MD-11 during a series of tests that culminated in the historic, first-ever landing of a throttles-only-controlled airliner. This event occurred at Edwards

Air Force Base on August 29, 1995. Engineers expect the PCA system to remain as a safety back-up feature in twenty-first century designs.

MD-10 Freighter

Just like the DC-8 before it, the DC-10 was destined to survive well beyond its originally expected life span by becoming an excellent freighter. Federal Express, which already operated a fleet of DC-10 and MD-11 freighters, announced an

agreement with DAC in September 1996 to convert a minimum of 60 DC-10s to MD-10s. The program was divided into two major phases, the first of which involved the conversion of ex-airline DC-10s into a freighter configuration. FedEx had already been busy buying up aircraft from American and United, and conversions on the first of these got under way in early 1997.

The second, more complex phase involved the installation of the advanced common flightdeck (ACF). This converted the traditional, three-crew cockpit of the trijet into a two-crew flightdeck like that of the MD-11. Indeed the ACF, which was based on Honeywell's VIA 2000 versatile integrated avionics architecture, took the MD-10 one step beyond the flightdeck of the MD-11 and even the Boeing 777. The MD-10 flightdeck featured six 8-inch flat panel displays and improved functionality. Triple VIA computers controlled the system, which supported satellite communications, GPS navigation, and other advances expected to be necessary in the future air traffic environment.

While the aircraft are being modified with the flightdeck changes, other structural upgrades will be made to increase the maximum takeoff weight. For the MD-10-10F, this weight will rise to 446,000 pounds with a payload of 143,500 pounds for a nonstop range of about 2,000 nautical miles. The MD-10-30F, on the other hand, will see its maximum takeoff weight increase to 580,000 pounds, providing payload capacity of 163,000 pounds over a range of up to 3,700 nautical miles.

Together with its existing DC-10 aircraft, Federal Express had orders and options for the conversion of up to 120 MD-10s. This application marks the beginning of yet another chapter in the long history of the world's most successful wide-body trijet.

A Pakistan International Airlines DC-10-30 is readied for departure at Karachi in January 1986. Twelve years after entering service with PIA (and only four months after this image was captured), the DC-10 was sold to Canadian Pacific Airlines, which named it *Empress of Tokyo*. With the demise of CP Air, it became part of the Canadian Airlines International fleet before flying for a period under lease to VASP of Brazil. By the mid-1990s, 20 years after it had rolled off the Long Beach line, it was flying for Continental Airlines.

MD-80:
SECOND GENERATION TWIN

The MD-80 was of critical importance to DAC for more than two decades. It was the first Douglas-designed jetliner, and only the fourth commercial jet to achieve sales of more than 1,000 units, following the Boeing 707, 727, and 737. By the time the last one rolls out in the year 2000, the MD-80 will have been produced continuously for 20 years.

In the long-established Douglas tradition of refining existing products rather than developing entirely new ones, the MD-80 emerged as a derivative of the DC-9. The company's studies were driven by the availability of a new Pratt & Whitney JT8D engine, which had a larger bypass ratio than the "straight eights" used on the basic DC-9 series. The engine offered the potential for growth beyond the largest DC-9 variant, the Series 50.

Supported largely by Swissair, which wanted more capacity on its European routes, the studies concentrated on a stretch of the Series 50. The concepts were variously known as the Series 55, the Series 50RSS (re-fanned Super Stretch), and the Series 60. By August 1977, the design was firming up around the Series 55 proposal. It had also become clear that, with a projected time of entry into service around 1980, DAC marketers should take advantage of the timing by calling the new project the DC-9 Series 80.

Because the new model was tailored to Swissair's requirement, it was no surprise when the airline launched it into production with an order for 15 firm and five options in October 1977. Austrian Airlines also ordered eight firm, while U.S. operator Southern Airways, later merged to form Republic, ordered four. Venezuelan carrier LAV also signed a letter of intent for three, although they were never taken up. The Southern Airways aircraft were also subsequently canceled.

Compared to the DC-9 Series 50, the Series 80 was extended 12 feet, 8 inches forward of the wing and 1 foot, 7 inches aft. The greater forward extension was required to maintain the center of gravity with the much heavier JT8D-200 version. The extended fuselage provided space for between 135 and 172 passengers, depending on configuration. As a result, the Series 80 had an overall length of 147 feet, 10 inches, compared to 133 feet, 6 inches for the Series 50. The actual passenger cabin from cockpit door to aft bulkhead was an impressive 101 feet long, just 1 foot shorter than the original DC-8 Series 10 cabin, and it retained the DC-9's 10-foot, 1-inch width.

Significant changes were also made to the wing, in order to support the optional maximum takeoff weight of 142,000 pounds, and to provide adequate field performance for the bigger aircraft.

This American Airlines MD-82 clearly displays its DC-9 heritage. The aircraft is one of 260 bought by the airline in the biggest single-model deal in jetliner history. Note the relatively large intakes of the Pratt & Whitney JT8D-217s, each capable of pumping out 20,000 pounds of thrust. The engines also have an extra 850 pounds of thrust in emergency reserve power.

A Chinese-made MD-82 makes a splendid sight as it turns an infamous corner to land at Hong Kong's Kai Tak shortly before the airport was closed in 1998. Built by Shanghai Aviation Industrial Corporation from kits sent over by Douglas, this aircraft was delivered to China Northern in March 1990. Although McDonnell Douglas pioneered important relationships like this one with the Chinese, both Boeing and Airbus ended up selling more aircraft to Chinese airlines.

Instead of performing major surgery on the wing and effectively redesigning the airfoil, DAC designers opted for the simplest solution of inserting a new section at the root and a larger tip. This made the wing 28 percent larger than the DC-9's and increased the area to 1,209 square feet. The extra space in the root enlarged fuel capacity to 5,480 gallons, giving the aircraft a typical range of 1,565 nautical miles with a load of 155 passengers. Although it featured the same 24.5-degree sweep as the earlier wing, the new 5-foot, 3-inch root extension and the 2-foot wingtip increased the Series 80 span to 107 feet, 10 inches.

The re-fanned JT8D was prompted by the success of the JT3D and Pratt & Whitney's realization that the bypass ratio of the first JT8D series was too low for upcoming noise and fuel economy requirements. Working with NASA, the company developed a new low pressure system that was added to the original high pressure core of the JT8D. The new single-stage fan, retained in subsequent versions with increased airflow, pumped almost 470 pounds of air per second in the first version, the JT8D-209. This was roughly 120 pounds per second more air than the initial JT8D engines had pumped. The bypass ratio therefore climbed to 1.78:1, compared to just over 1 for the straight JT8D. The improvement boosted efficiency and cut noise dramatically. Overall pressure ratio was increased with a new, six-stage low pressure compressor, or "core booster" as P&W called it.

The first -209 engine was flight-tested on the YC-15 transport on March 4, 1977. It was commercially launched later that month with the go-ahead of the Series 80. The engine was certificated by the FAA in June 1979. It had an initial rating of

The clean lines of an SAS MD-81 reveal the 14-foot, 3-inch fuselage extension that makes this model look much longer than the DC-9-50. The 5-foot, 3-inch wing root plugs and the 2-foot tip extensions are also clearly visible as *Albin Viking* sets course from London's Heathrow airport toward the Land of the Midnight Sun.

Alitalia's MD-82 *Viesta* climbs into a late-summer European sky en route to Italy. With maximum takeoff weights of up to 149,500 pounds, the MD-82 has a typical range of 2,050 nautical miles when carrying 155 passengers.

18,500 pounds of thrust at 25 degrees Celsius, with an emergency single-engine thrust rating of 19,250 pounds. In tandem with DAC's growth plan for the Series 80, P&W also developed a family of more powerful -200s. The first off the mark was the -217, rated at 20,000 pounds thrust. It was followed by the -219, which had a thrust rating of 21,000 pounds.

Enter the MD-80

The first Series 80, still officially referred to as a DC-9 at this stage, made its first flight on October 19, 1979. The subsequent test program was a success, despite two significant incidents. Both events, one at Edwards Air Force Base and the other at Yuma, involved high sink rate landings. Both resulted in structural damage to the test aircraft. The aircraft's design was altered slightly as a consequence.

The first version was designated the DC-9-81. Despite the incidents, it was approved under an amended FAA DC-9 Type Certificate after a test program that involved three aircraft, 1,085 flight hours, and 795 flights. The first delivery to Swissair took place on September 13, 1980. This plane entered commercial service just under a month later, when it operated a flight from Zurich to London Heathrow.

Meanwhile, work was under way on several variants, the first of which was the Series 82. This design incorporated the more powerful -217 engine, then under development by Pratt & Whitney, which would offer better hot and high performance. The Series 82 was identical to the Series 81 in most other respects. It had a slightly higher maximum takeoff weight of 147,000 pounds, which was later increased to 149,500 pounds. In standard operations, the range of the Series 82 was therefore slightly better than that of

Avianca's route network allows it to make good use of the extended-range MD-83, which can carry 155 passengers up to 2,500 nautical miles. Note the striped pattern on the inboard upper wing surface. This provides visual warning of any ice buildup on the surface of the wing fuel tank's "cold corner." Ice shedding from this area led to the crash of one MD-80.

An MD-83 belonging to German charter operator Aero Lloyd lands at Palma, Majorca, with a service from Europe. To get the longer range, the MD-83 is fitted with two auxiliary fuel tanks in the cargo compartment fore and aft of the wing center section. Each of the auxiliary tanks holds 580 U.S. gallons of fuel. This increases total fuel capacity to almost 6,940 U.S. gallons, compared to 5,780 U.S. gallons in the standard MD-80.

Smoking tires mark the moment of touchdown for an American Airlines MD-82 at Dallas-Fort Worth. This reverse-angle look at the aircraft shows the hydraulically actuated double-slotted flaps, which cover 67 percent of the span. The MD-82 was delivered to American in July 1985.

the earlier model. It could carry 155 passengers up to 2,050 nautical miles.

The Series 82 was launched in April 1979 with an order from Aeromexico. In reality Inex Adria, the forerunner of today's Adria Airways, could be considered the launch customer because it ordered three generic Series 80 aircraft in August 1978. Two of these turned out to be Series 82s when delivered. The first aircraft (line number 996) flew on January 8, 1981, and was certificated by the FAA on July 29 of the same year. The first production aircraft was subsequently delivered to Republic on August 5, 1981, entering service later that month.

As had happened with all previous Douglas jetliners, the airlines soon began asking for longer-range versions of the Series 80. The initial result was the Series 83, which was fitted with two 565-gallon auxiliary fuel tanks in the belly, located fore and aft of the wing center section. The extra fuel increased maximum takeoff weight to 160,000 pounds. It boosted range with 155 passengers to about 2,500 nautical miles. Heavier weight resulted in numerous changes to the landing gear, wheels, tires, and brakes. The wing and floor beams were also beefed-up. The wing skin was thickened; the front spar web and the elevator spar cap were also strengthened. The changes were originally tailored specifically to the long-range Series 83, but from line number 1194 (a Series 81) forward, all aircraft incorporated the heavier structure.

The advent of the Series 83 in January 1983 heralded a turning point for the program, and for DAC in general. Beginning in late 1982, all DC-9-80 Series aircraft were marketed as

Although pilots must exercise caution to avoid scraping the tail of the lengthened MD-80 on takeoff and landing, this apparent near-collision with the ground is actually an optical illusion. The visual distortion is caused by the proximity of the parallel runway at Seatac International Airport. Note the prominent, low-drag "beaver" tail cone fairing on the Alaska Airlines MD-83, which was delivered in April 1995.

MD-80s. This presented the twinjet as a more modern project, distancing it from the DC-9. It also recognized the stewardship of McDonnell Douglas for the first time, beginning a new classification system that would remain in existence until the company's name disappeared forever in 1998. Production of DC-9s therefore officially concluded in late 1982, after the delivery of 976 DC-9s and 108 DC-9 Series 80s. The MD-80s officially began in December of that year with the 1,085th DC-9/MD-80, which was an MD-82 built for VIASA. More importantly at the time, the MD-83 also stimulated sales, which had been very poor for the first five years of the program's life.

The company had taken fewer than 100 orders during that time period.

Part of the transformation was due to a daring "walk away" lease deal struck with American Airlines over the MD-82. Under the terms of the deal, American was not bound by any contract in the traditional way. It could literally walk away from taking new aircraft if industry conditions changed for the worse. The gamble more than paid off, as both American and TWA built up fleets of MD-80s. Over the years, American took a staggering 260 MD-82s. On June 11, 1992, American took one of its last few aircraft deliveries. This plane, N596AA, was the 2,000th twinjet built by DAC.

DAC continued to study and develop new derivatives throughout the 1980s, attempting to exploit every possible niche. The last and most significantly different MD-80 variant produced as a result of these studies was the MD-87. The aircraft was shortened by 17 feet, 4 inches, to just over 130 feet. It could provide seating for 114 passengers in a typical mixed-class arrangement, but it retained the engines, systems, and flight deck of the other MD-80 family members. To compensate for the shorter fuselage and the resulting reduced moment arm, the fin cap above the "T" of the tail was made taller. A new low-drag tail cone, which resembled the flattened tail of a beaver, was also developed for the aircraft. The -87 achieved a 0.5-percent improvement in fuel burn as a result. The improvements were so good that from 1987 forward, the "beaver" tail cone was introduced on the other MD-80 variants and was retrofitted to models built earlier.

The only MD-80 version to be shortened was the MD-87. Here an -87 shares the ramp at Osaka's Itami airport with a YS-11 turboprop and a newly delivered company MD-90. The specially extended fin cap, developed to compensate for the shorter moment arm of the MD-87, was later adapted for use on the MD-90 and the 717-200.

The MD-87 was formally launched in January 1985 on the back of orders placed the previous December by Austrian and Finnair. The first aircraft (line number 1326) emerged from the Long Beach factory on October 23, 1986, and flew on December 4 of that year. The changes incorporated into the MD-87 necessitated a longer certification effort, so the first aircraft was not handed over to Finnair until November 1, 1987. Ultimately, a total of 76 MD-87s were built. The development aircraft was retained as a test aircraft by DAC for more than a decade. The last MD-87 (line number 1985) was handed over to SAS in March 1992.

Another minor derivative was the MD-88, which was essentially identical to the MD-82/83.

However, the flight deck incorporated an electronic flight instrument system (EFIS) display in place of the more conventional instrument display. It also had an upgraded interior and a windshear warning system, the latter becoming an option available on all MD-80s. Although the changes were not huge, launch customer Delta saw them as significant enough to warrant a new designation. The model was launched in January 1986 on the back of orders for 80. The first MD-88 (line number 1395) flew on August 15, 1987, and entered service with Delta in January 1988.

As a result of new derivatives, an improving economy, and initiatives like the MD-83 lease deals, sales jumped sharply from 1983 forward,

Is it a jet or is it a prop? This unconventional, ultra-high bypass unducted fan (UDF) was developed by General Electric in response to successive increases in fuel prices and growing concerns about noise. Although considered a technical success, the 22,700-pound-thrust GE36 propfan was shelved after negative airline reaction and a return to stable fuel prices. It is seen here mounted on a McDonnell Douglas-owned MD-80 testbed at the 1988 Farnborough air show.

TWA's surprise 1998 order for 24 MD-83s helped extend the life of the twinjet production line into the year 2000. MD-90s are shown in the background, and the first 717-200s can be seen at the far end of Building 80. Boeing hoped these planes would soon replace the other twins on this historic production line.

averaging around 125 per year for the rest of the decade. The biggest single year was 1989, when 268 aircraft were ordered.

However, the fortunes of the MD-80, along with the rest of Douglas, would dip dramatically in the 1990s, with the onset of a severe economic depression. The situation was worsened by a crisis in the Middle East, triggered by Iraq's invasion of Kuwait. Although the production line was still busy coping with the backlog, reaching a peak of 12 aircraft built per month in 1991, sales dropped to 60 in 1990 and only 27 in 1991. To make matters worse, some 66 existing orders were canceled, cutting the net order book total to 1,137, or 14 less than the year-end figure for the previous year. The MD-80's slide was exacerbated by the emergence of DAC's own MD-90, but the primary

problem was stiff competition from Boeing and the Airbus A320 family.

Despite major efforts by DAC, which managed to remain profitable with dramatically reduced production numbers, the amount of MD-80 work tailed off throughout the mid-1990s. By the time of the Boeing takeover in August 1997, termination of the line had become inevitable. Although a 1999 end date was announced, the industry was surprised when TWA placed an order for 24 MD-83s in April 1998. The work provided a much-needed boost for the Long Beach employees, who faced massive layoffs as a result of the closure decision. However, the TWA order only delayed the inevitable. MD-80 production ends with the delivery of the 1,160th aircraft, marking the completion of DAC's most successful jetliner program.

5

MD-11: ULTIMATE TRIJET

The massive MD-11 was the largest jetliner that ever emerged from the DAC stable. As a stretched derivative of the DC-10, it is likely to remain not only the biggest wide-body trijet ever built, but also the last. Hampered in early life by performance problems, it later went on to exceed its original targets and became the platform for one of the world's most successful large freighters.

The roots of the MD-11 go back to 1978, when the company was furiously negotiating the KC-10A contract. DAC planners knew that, even if the KC-10A work came through, the end of the current DC-10 family was in sight. Airlines were still keen on the trijet concept, however, and continued to search for more range and capacity. Following the lead of the DC-8 evolution, the company therefore sketched out three new DC-10 derivatives, dubbing these the Series 61, Series 62, and Series 63. They planned to stretch the -61 and -63 by 40 feet, while the -62 would feature a shorter stretch of just under 27 feet. The Series 61 was aimed at U.S. domestic routes and would use the basic DC-10 wing. The Series 62 traded airframe weight for range. With a larger span wing, it would have greater range than the other two. The Series 63 design combined the long fuselage of the -61 with the bigger wing of the -62, providing a large-capacity, medium- to long-haul jet.

Like many DAC projects before it, the stretched DC-10 concept was the victim of unfortunate timing. World recession overwhelmed the industry, in the late 1970s, and the plans were shelved. Three years later, design engineers refocused briefly on an advanced-technology trijet, the MD-100. Although roughly equivalent to the DC-10, the MD-100 incorporated new technology systems with a two-crew cockpit and the same second-generation, high-bypass-ratio engines that were being used on the Boeing 757. But the MD-100 failed to attract much interest from the airlines. By November 1983, it had been abandoned.

Despite its cancellation, the MD-100 concept played a vital role. It helped DAC focus on the benefits of the newest propulsion and system technologies. It made the company aware of the potential benefits of injecting these new technologies into the original DC-10-30 design. Thus, in July 1984, DAC announced the MD-XXX. This aircraft was a radical revamping of the DC-10-30, incorporating modern engines (the GE CF6-80C2 or the Pratt & Whitney PW4000) and several system improvements. One version of the MD-XXX featured a 22-foot, 3-inch stretch, and this version was to provide the foundation for the MD-11.

The MD-XXX quickly matured into the conceptual basis for a whole new family, which DAC

Under a threatening French summer sky, a Federal Express MD-11 taxis past members of the enormous rabbit population at Charles de Gaulle Airport. FedEx fell in love with the MD-11, and began buying up ex-American machines as well as new production versions. The company even acquired the prototype MD-11 after the completion of flight tests.

The sheer length of the MD-11, the largest Douglas jetliner ever developed, is revealed in this view of an American Airlines aircraft taxiing at London Heathrow. The General Electric CF6-80C2-powered version is slightly longer overall, measuring 201 feet, 4 inches because of an extended tail engine mounting unit. By comparison, the Pratt & Whitney PW4000 versions are 200 feet, 11 inches long.

christened the MD-11X. The first version, the MD-11X-10ER, was essentially a DC-10-30. The other two versions, the MD-11X-20 and the MD-100X-MR, had longer fuselages. If program launch occurred by mid-1985, DAC predicted that deliveries would begin in 1989. Sure enough, in July 1985, the McDonnell Douglas board authorized the presentation of firm MD-11 proposals to airlines. The schedule now called for launch by early 1986, with deliveries starting in late 1989. Company marketers correctly predicted a market for up to 1,400 aircraft in this size class by 1998. However, they were wrong when they predicted that DAC would sell more than 300 of these aircraft.

Go-Ahead

The giant trijet got the official go-ahead on December 30, 1986, on the back of orders and commitments for 92 aircraft from 12 airlines and leasing companies. These customers included British Caledonian, SAS, Dragonair, and Mitsui.

The aircraft had meanwhile shrunk slightly compared to the original plan. It was effectively stretched by inserting an 8-foot, 4-inch plug forward of the wing and another 10-foot, 2-inch plug aft. This created a total stretch of 18 feet, 6 inches, some 4 feet shorter than the initial MD-11X concept. Otherwise, the plan had not changed. It featured 58,000-pound-thrust engines, a modernized interior, and an all-new two-crew cockpit.

Even at this embryonic stage, the MD-11 was slipping behind schedule. Scheduling problems would plague the aircraft one way or another throughout its short production life. Launch had been delayed by almost one year, in order to secure enough firm commitments. By the end of 1987, a sense of unease pervaded the program. The orders had come in slowly, with just 30 firm. None of DAC's large, traditional U.S. customers, like American and Delta, had placed any orders.

But the news was not all gloomy. Some business trickled in when Alitalia ordered the first

MD-11 Combi (a combination passenger/freighter) in April 1987. The following month, the first MD-11F freighter was ordered by Federal Express, which marked the beginning of a long association between the trijet and the express carrier. But the big orders had not materialized, so DAC began a series of new development studies to stimulate more interest. These included an Advanced (later known as Super) Stretch with a 35-foot fuselage extension and a panorama deck. The panorama deck was offered as an insertable module, providing seating for up to 62 in the forward cargo area below the main deck.

Assembly of the first aircraft began on March 9, 1988. The first flight was scheduled for about a year later. The start of construction provided new impetus to the program, which was stimulated again in June when Rolls-Royce signed an agreement to offer the RB211-524L engine, later

renamed the Trent 665. The 65,500-pound-thrust engine was the first non-domestic engine offered on a Douglas jetliner since the Conway RCO.12 Mk 509 had been offered on the DC-8 thirty years earlier (see chapter 1). However, the new association with Rolls-Royce proved all too brief. The option was dropped in 1991 when Air Europe, the sole customer for the version, ceased operations.

There was more bad news to come. The ramp-up in MD-11 work coincided with significant increases on the MD-80 line, as well as serious development work on what was soon to emerge as the MD-90. DAC was being stretched financially. To make matters worse, suppliers were failing to adhere to their schedules. As a result, DAC slipped its first flight to April 1989. Even this turned out to be optimistic, as further problems hit the program. Like Boeing with the 747-400, DAC was paying the price for trying to develop too many

Delta tackled long-range performance shortfalls in its early aircraft, like this MD-11 delivered in November 1992. The company's solution involved installing two auxiliary fuel tanks in the rear freight hold. These provided an extra 3,948 U.S. gallons, increasing the total capacity to 44,131 U.S. gallons.

Humid air condenses explosively over the heavily loaded wing of the Alitalia MD-11 *Gioachino Rossini* as it begins its initial climb after takeoff. Note the clearly outlined aluminum and carbon fiber winglets, which extend 7 feet above the wing and 2 feet, 6 inches below, as well as the tightly formed vortex spinning off the engine-mounted strake.

options virtually at once. With a large number of different engine/airframe combinations coming down the line, a huge new workforce to train, and more supplier problems, DAC bowed to the inevitable by announcing further delays. Roll out did not occur until November 6, 1989, and first flight took place on January 10, 1990—roughly eight months late.

There was some good news on the order book side of the ledger. Orders had finally started to accelerate. The big breakthrough came in September 1988, when Delta ordered nine firm plus 31 options. The following February produced a bumper harvest of orders, including business from Air Zaire, Finnair, Garuda, and Aero Lloyd. The biggest single deal also came in that month, in the shape of an order for eight with 42 options from American. Singapore Airlines (SIA) also placed a vital order for 20 in 1990. This further enhanced the program's credibility.

Performance Problems

The MD-11 was certificated as a derivative of the DC-10 on November 30, 1990, after a flight test effort involving five aircraft and almost 2,000 flight hours. A hand-over ceremony for the first aircraft delivered to Finnair was held one day before certification was granted, so contracts were formally exchanged on December 7. Finnair's first revenue service with the trijet occurred on December 20, when the aircraft carried vacationers from Helsinki to Tenerife in the Canary Islands.

Although the test program had gone smoothly, the results of the long-range flight tests that took place toward the end of that effort worried DAC. Detailed analysis of data from these tests revealed disturbing performance shortfalls. The aircraft had been marketed with a range of 6,840 to 7,000 nautical miles when carrying 293 passengers and bags. Data from proving flights suggested that, with a 61,000-pound payload, the P&W-powered

An Alitalia MD-11 Combi *Valle dei Templi* makes the tight final turn toward Hong Kong's Kai Tak airport in late 1997. Alitalia was the launch customer for the Combi, which is fitted with a 160-inch by 102-inch main deck cargo door on the port side aft of the wing. The Combi can carry up to 60,000 pounds of freight and 214 passengers in a two-class layout.

MD-11 would run out of steam at around 6,270 nautical miles. The GE version fared little better, attaining a maximum range of only 6,460 nautical miles. DAC immediately began asking questions. Was it the engines? The weight of the airframe? Too much drag? Unfortunately, the answer implicated all three.

Most of the problems stemmed from the engines, whose makers appeared to have been overzealous in their performance expectations and promises. Apart from the 747, the MD-11 was the only widebody in production with more than two power plants and a choice of engines. This made it an attractive market for the engine makers. Performance guarantees were made to DAC and the airlines, but the guarantees were not met. Fuel burn on the PW4460-powered version was 6.7 to 8.4 percent above contract specification, while the CF6-80C2D1F was 4.5 to 5.3 percent above the limit. The horrible truth began to dawn on DAC. The company angrily withheld contract payments to the engine makers and to General Dynamics, which had made the fuselage sections in San Diego, for failing to meet performance guarantees.

While the engine manufacturers began a hurried "get well" program to reduce the fuel burn of their power plants, DAC rushed into a rigorous performance improvement program (PIP) of its own. The company's three-point plan addressed drag, weight, and fuel in an effort to get the

Despite the increasing trend away from passenger versions of the MD-11, the trijet reigned supreme as a freighter. With a 140-inch by 102-inch main deck side cargo door, it could load up to 35 freight pallets and carry 156,000 pounds of payload on the main deck. This Federal Express MD-11 was delivered in August 1993.

MD-11 back into line with its performance expectations. The company knew it did not have a moment to lose. Airbus was into the fourth year of its competing A340 development effort, and Boeing had just launched the 777. The result at DAC was the A-1 PIP, which reduced drag by 0.7 percent in Phase I through the addition of splitter plates, which resembled a tiny projecting ledge on the trailing edge of the wing. Phase II, introduced in

mid-1993 as A-1 Package 1, saw a 1.5-percent drag reduction and a 100-nautical-mile range increase or 2,500-pound payload improvement. Phase II involved drooping the outer ailerons by three degrees in the cruise to improve span loading. It also entailed adding slat seals to the outer slat segments.

A-1 Package 2 involved beefing up the wing box structure, the leading and trailing edges, and the undercarriage in order to take the heavier

A Swissair MD-11 rotates smoothly for take-off en-route to Zurich from California. The aircraft's perfect record with Swissair was tragically broken in September 1998 with the crash of a sister ship off the coast of Newfoundland. Investigators found signs of heat damage and suspected fire as the cause of the crash. The Swissair fleet was earmarked for sale to Fedex which, as of early 1999, was the only other operator to suffer an MD-11 crash when it lost an aircraft in a non-fatal incident in July 1997.

weight, which was boosted from 618,000 pounds to 625,000 pounds. This increased fuel-carrying capacity and added 250 nautical miles to the range or 7,000 pounds to the payload.

The A-1 Package 3 saw a re-rigging of the inboard and outboard ailerons, enabling them to droop for takeoff. This improved takeoff performance at higher maximum takeoff weights and coincided with new aerodynamic refinements that were introduced with Phase IIIA of the PIP. The latter was introduced in mid-1993, resulting in a 1-percent drag improvement. Again the drag reductions were produced by very minor changes, such as a pylon fillet, seals around the ailerons, and a windshield fairing.

Phase IIIB, introduced in late 1994, resulted in another improvement of 1.5 percent. The changes included increasing the diameter of the number two intake, one of the few upgrades that was not retrofittable. Phase IV, which came in February 1995, virtually completed the recovery by producing a further 1.2-percent drag reduction. It included a re-rigged elevator, a wing and undercarriage seal package, and a redesigned flap hinge fairing. All in all, the PIP produced an 8-percent improvement in performance, restoring the range to 7,000 nautical miles with 298 passengers. Modifications also included increased fuel capacity via either extended standard tanks or modular add-on tanks in the cargo bay for seasonal head winds.

Unlike all other aspects of the enlarged MD-11 design, the horizontal tailplane actually shrank in comparison to the DC-10 unit. Its span was reduced from 71 feet, 2 inches to 59 feet, 2 inches. Its total area decreased proportionately from 1,338 square feet to 920 square feet. The slightly stubby nature of the design is illustrated on this Japan Air Lines "J Bird" MD-11, which was delivered in December 1993.

Meanwhile, the engine makers' PIP efforts produced fuel burn improvements of up to 3 percent, creating savings of up to $300,000 per aircraft per year in fuel bills.

Ups and Downs

Despite the desperate rush to rebuild the performance of the aircraft, airline confidence was badly dented by the shortfall revelations. The program took its biggest single hit on August 2, 1991. On that day Singapore Airlines, a prestigious customer, announced that it was canceling its MD-11 order

and would instead take up to 20 Airbus A340-300s. SIA had ordered MD-11s specifically for its extensive network of long, thin routes, such as the 7,200-nautical-mile Singapore to Paris sector. Because the performance shortfall made such missions impossible, particularly in winter head wind conditions, the order was canceled. SIA's decision sent reverberations throughout the airline world and marked the beginning of the end for the MD-11.

Despite the setback, DAC continued to streamline its production processes. It developed PIPs, produced an increasing number of freighters and convertibles, and, in hopes of extending the family, the company began studying more derivatives. These included a growth MD-11 dubbed the MD-12X. This concept gradually mutated into a double-deck, four-engine 747 replacement, which would be built in close cooperation with Taiwan. After this venture failed, DAC returned to more conservative derivatives. The "panorama deck" study was revived, as was an MD-11 Twin design whose origin could be traced back to a similar option considered for the DC-10. The last derivative to actually see the light of day was the MD-11ER, which featured increased range and payload with auxiliary fuel tanks and a higher maximum takeoff weight. DAC delivered the first MD-11ER, which

was also the company's ultimate trijet, to World Airways in early 1996.

The next and final proposed development of the aircraft was the MD-XX. This concept returned to the stretched fuselage, but it differed from virtually all previous derivatives in that it featured a new wing. By this stage, in late 1995, airlines had begun questioning whether McDonnell Douglas would survive. Newly installed McDonnell Douglas president Harry Stonecipher offered reassurances. "If we weren't already in the jetliner business," he said, "we'd get into it." Nevertheless, confidence in the company's future was at an all-time low. After DAC's many previous false-starts and proposals, the airlines were equally

A China Eastern MD-11F climbs sharply after takeoff. Including the lower cargo deck payload, this aircraft's maximum capacity exceeds 200,000 pounds. Typical range with a payload of 194,600 pounds is more than 3,630 nautical miles.

A peek up the empty tail engine housing on a late-model MD-11 reveals the enormous "banjo" fitting and the cantilevered strut, which will support the number two engine in place. The shiny, low-drag tail cone hinges down for engine removal. So do the inboard elevator sections, which are shown in their drooped position. The building's low truss height prevents workers from fitting the vertical tail until near the end of the assembly process, which is completed outside.

wing, which had its roots firmly in the 1960s. The 40-percent increase in wing area meant that both medium- to long-range and very long-range versions could be developed at the same time. DAC forecast a market for up to 2,500 aircraft, split almost evenly between the two versions, and predicted entry into service by December 2000. American and Swissair were among the airlines "extremely interested," said DAC in September 1996. By this time it had received letters of interest from six airlines for a total of 40 aircraft.

Everything hinged on a McDonnell Douglas board meeting in St. Louis in October 1996. DAC was optimistic that it would at last be given the go-ahead to develop a true giant in the DC-8 mold that would be available for the right market at the right time. They were badly disappointed. The board canceled the MD-XX.

The airlines were now unsure that DAC could support its own products, let alone develop new ones. Worse still, McDonnell Douglas itself had lost a succession of major space and defense contracts, including the vital Joint StrikeFighter. It was being backed into a tight corner in areas that it had previously dominated. Left in a mire, with limited prospects but huge resources, McDonnell Douglas went in search of a partner.

The fallout was a much speculated upon but previously unthinkable merger with the mighty Boeing company. After being arch rivals for so long, the two biggest names in American aerospace were formally merged under the Boeing name in August 1997. The MD-11 was a surprise survivor of a product strategy review in November of that year. By this time, the aircraft's inherent strengths as a freighter had become apparent, attracting orders from Lufthansa as late as September 1996. By throwing its marketing strength behind the product, Boeing hoped to stimulate additional freighter sales.

Here is a classic view of the last few MD-11s moving slowly down the Long Beach line in the late 1990s. This vast assembly area was once home to the DC-10 line. Following Boeing's takeover, it was slated to be used for modification work. The last MD-11, a freighter for Lufthansa, is expected to come off the line in 2001.

skeptical about new variants of the MD-11. The company knew it was "now or never time," so it decided to go all out with a re-winged, stretched MD-11. This aircraft would provide a 747 replacement as well as an able, long-range competitor for newer versions of the A340 and the 777.

The newer, thicker wing had a span of 213 feet and was designed to fit in 747-sized gates. It could cruise higher, faster, and farther than the MD-11

In late 1997, the Long Beach delivery ramp briefly looked as it had in the glory days, as newly built freighters for Saudi Arabian and EVA Air stacked up.

After many false starts the closest Douglas came to reviving its long-term hopes for a future MD-11 successor was this project, the re-winged MD-XX. Unfortunately, the project was scrapped by the McDonnell Douglas board. This two-member family would have been perfectly positioned to attack the 747 replacement market in the year 2000. However, lack of investment and failing airline confidence in the future of Douglas gave the MDC board little choice. Within two months of the decision, merger talks with Boeing had begun.

Unfortunately, this did not happen. On June 3, 1998, the company announced that production of the MD-11 would be phased out, with the last delivery scheduled for February 2000. "Despite our best marketing efforts, it became clear to us that there simply wasn't enough customer interest in either the passenger or freighter versions of this airplane to justify keeping the production line open," said Ron Woodard, then president of Boeing Commercial Airplane Group. Within months, Lufthansa again came to the rescue by firming up three options and ordering three additional MD-11Fs. The extension meant MD-11 deliveries would continue until 2001.

So ended DAC's three decades of DC-10/MD-11 manufacturing. By the time the last one is delivered, a combined tally of more than 640 trijets is expected. Because the MD-11 has long outlasted its nearest rival, the Lockheed L-1011 TriStar, the final MD-11 will likely be the world's final newly built, wide-body trijet.

The ultimate Douglas jetliner was the MD-11ER, pictured here in the colors of World Airways. Complete with an array of aerodynamic improvements, engine enhancements, and 1,500 pounds of weight savings, the ER could fly more than 7,210 nautical miles with 323 passengers.

MD-90: LONGEST TWIN

The MD-90, launched in November 1989, is remarkable for being the longest rear-engined twin aircraft ever built. Powered by the International Aero Engines (IAE) V2500 turbofan, it was also quickly acknowledged as one of the quietest and most environmentally friendly aircraft in existence.

The roots of the MD-90 go back to at least 1979, when development of the MD-80 was well under way. The availability of the newly developed CFM56 high-bypass-ratio engine, plus an alternative study engine from Pratt & Whitney (the STF-517), gave Douglas designers new options. They could now stretch the -80 by another 9 feet, 6 inches. The extra length provided three more seat rows and balanced the aircraft against the heavier weight of the bigger engines, which could produce up to 25,000 pounds of thrust.

The stretch MD-80 was particularly advocated by CFM International, a joint company established by General Electric and Snecma of France in order to develop the CFM56. CFMI was desperate for business. It also pushed the new engine at Boeing, which began similar studies aimed at re-engining the 737 in 1979. These studies led to the launch of the 737-300 in March 1981, and ultimately triggered a Boeing 737 dynasty that chalked up its 4,000th sale in 1998. The CFM56 completely transformed the 737 and its fortunes. In doing so, it added to the pressures that would later see the MD-90 canceled before its time.

With all this well ahead, DAC faced the more imminent pressure of certificating the MD-80. The company opted to focus on smaller versions rather than larger ones. The first reference to a "Super 90" thus referred to a short-bodied MD-80, which DAC believed would be ideal for the deregulated U.S. air transport industry of the 1980s. Development of the Super 90 was curtailed, however, by the ensuing recession. New developments of the MD-80 were put on ice until the economic recovery began in the mid-1980s.

The short-bodied MD-80 finally emerged as the MD-87 (see chapter 4), while the stretched version once again re-entered the frame, this time as the MD-89. The new stretch measured 160 feet, 6 inches in length, making it longer than anything previously proposed. It would be 12 feet, 8 inches longer than the basic MD-80. It could seat up to 173 passengers and would have a takeoff weight of 155,000 pounds. Significantly, it was to be powered by either the CFM56 or the competing V2500, which was being developed by International Aero Engines. This international consortium included Pratt & Whitney, Rolls-Royce, Japanese Aero Engine Corporation, MTU of Germany, and Fiat of Italy. The Roman numeral V in V2500 represented the five partners. However, Fiat withdrew in 1996 and its shares were evenly redistributed.

By now the CFM56 had secured positions on the A320 and 737 aircraft. IAE, meanwhile,

Europe has some of the toughest environmental rules in the world which helped secure a sale of MD-90s to SAS, because of the low emissions of the IAE V2500 engine. Here the relatively large diameter of the turbofans is apparent as an SAS MD-90 nears touchdown.

The first MD-90 "T-1" leaves Mojave, California, on a test flight in April 1993. The empennage is covered with tufts, enabling flight test engineers to visualize aerodynamic flow over the tail area. The large, engine-mounted strake, seen clearly here, was dramatically reduced in size as a result of these and other tests.

was in the same position CFMI had been in six years earlier. It desperately needed an application for its engine. Negotiations with DAC intensified and, on February 1, 1985, McDonnell Douglas announced that it would begin joint marketing of a V2500-powered MD-80. The future of the program was, however, far from certain. DAC was very interested in a new-generation propfan engine, also known as an unducted fan engine. The new generation had been spurred by the latest oil crisis (see the UHB demonstrator picture, chapter 4).

The low fuel consumption and supposed noise benefits of these unusual engines could not be ignored, so the company outlined plans for two new versions of the MD-80. One was the MD-91, which was a propfan-powered, MD-87-sized aircraft. The other was an MD-80-sized version dubbed the MD-92. In the meantime, DAC also planned to begin designing an all-new, propfan-powered aircraft called the MD-94.

Events once more conspired against DAC's bold initiatives. The world oil supply stabilized. Fuel prices dropped, and technical issues began cropping up with the new engines. Even passenger acceptance of the rather bizarre-looking propfans was questioned, and the concept was quietly dropped. By 1988, with the propfans already destined for museums, DAC once more turned its attention to conventional turbofans.

Key to the entire MD-90 effort was the 25,000-pound-thrust, high-bypass V2500 power plant made by International Aero Engines. The wide chord fan blades, visible inside the inlet, were the first to be seen on any production Douglas jetliner engine. Note the trailing cone, which was used by the test engineers to determine static air pressure outside the aircraft. This enabled them to calibrate the instruments mounted on the MD-90.

The MD-90's rear-pylon platform area, seen as the slab-like structures supporting the engines, was enlarged to counter the danger of deep-stall, which is faced by all T-tail designs in the development stage. The crew had an emergency escape chute mounted on the tail stairway in case they needed to bail out. The stair was weighed down to speed deployment and was covered with a smooth sliding surface to help crew members shoot into the slipstream.

MD-90 Launch

The MD-90 was formally announced on October 10, 1989. It was given the firm go-ahead just over a month later on the back of a substantial order from Delta, which had traditionally been one of DAC's best customers. Delta's order for 50 firm and 110 options was followed by more sales during 1990. Customers included two leasing companies, ILFC and GATX, as well as Japan Air Service. All the orders were for the MD-90-30 version, although others were offered. These ranged from the 110-seat MD-90-10 to the 180-seat MD-90-40. DAC also briefly considered a retrofit version of the MD-80 with V2500s, which was dubbed the MD-90-20. Like many of the other proposed versions of the MD-90, it was never built.

The next big sales target was a once-loyal group of DAC customers, all of which had bought DC-9s and MD-80s. They included Austrian, Finnair, SAS, and Swissair, and they had formed the European Quality Alliance, which was looking for a total of up to 240 aircraft in the MD-90 size category. The order was so important that DAC offered a specially tailored variant, the MD-90EC (Enhanced Configuration). This version featured an improved interior, flight deck, cargo handling system, and payload/range, plus a higher maximum takeoff weight of 172,500 pounds.

The sales campaign went on throughout 1990, but DAC received bad news by the end of the year. It had lost the Austrian and Swissair orders to Airbus, which had sold these two carriers the A320/321. Although SAS had not yet committed to the A320, DAC decided to discontinue

the EC variant, which had been offered on both the -30 and the -40. Undeterred by events in Europe, DAC continued to study new versions with longer range. One variant that did become a reality was the -30ER (Extended Range), which was offered with auxiliary fuel tanks in the belly. These increased the maximum fuel volume to 42,900 pounds and the range to 2,172 nautical miles, while also increasing maximum takeoff weight to 168,000 pounds. This made it 12,000 pounds heavier than the standard MD-90. An interim higher gross weight version was also developed with a maximum takeoff weight of 166,000 pounds.

Impressive climb performance was an early hallmark of the MD-90. Here an aircraft belonging to Delta Air Lines accelerates away from Orange County Airport in California. Delta launched the program in November 1989 with orders and options for up to 160 aircraft, though most of these were never built.

Low noise and high capacity were two big reasons why Reno Air chose the MD-90 for its service to noise-sensitive Orange County from San Jose, Silicon Valley, and its base in Reno, Nevada. Here one of the airline's "Orange County Flier" MD-90s launches out of John Wayne, Orange County, in the summer of 1998, shortly before Reno Air was purchased by American Airlines.

The MD-XX study became a casualty of the rejection by Swissair and Austrian. This aircraft was an advanced twin with a conventional tail, but it used high-tech, fly-by-wire flight control and lightweight, composite materials. Originally aimed at the A321 size category, the MD-XX continued to evolve upward until preliminary designs ranged between 190 and 270 seats. If it had launched, the aircraft would have filled the large gap that existed in DAC's product range between the MD-90 and the MD-11. However, the twin MD-XX study fizzled out. The name was last used for the abortive stretched MD-11, which was canceled in October 1996 (see chapter 5).

DAC originally planned to convert the MD-80 prototype (line number 909) into the initial MD-90 for flight testing. But the company quickly realized that this would make certification nearly impossible, due to the sheer number of new features being considered for the more advanced aircraft. Instead, it decided to proceed immediately with a purpose-built MD-90 prototype and move forward with advanced production of the aircraft at the same time.

Faced with enormous pressure to modernize its relatively dated and costly production methods, DAC took the opportunity with the MD-90 to completely change the way it built and designed its

Two MD-90s destined for JAS sit alongside an MD-80 and a preserved DC-2 on the Long Beach delivery ramp. Between them, the new MD-90s and the ancient DC-2 span 63 years of continuous aerospace development at Douglas.

products. Electronic product definition (EPD) was one improvement. Using computers (Hewlett-Packard hardware and Unigraphics II software), engineers would create solid models from drawings and use these models to produce electronic mock-ups. They then used the mockups for designing new parts and checking for interference before any part was released for manufacture.

"The MD-90 was an interesting place to start, because it was somewhat of a low risk," said EPD business unit manager Peter Swanson in 1992. The unit began by focusing on the new parts, such as the pylon for the V2500 engine. Next it concentrated on the wing, hoping that its study would later benefit the MD-95 program, which was following close behind.

DAC also developed a modular concept for the production of major fuselage sections. The eventual goal, realized in 1993, was to create interchangeable, standardized fuselage sections common to both the MD-80 and the MD-90. Don Hoisington was the general manager of the MD-90 production line at the time. According to Hoisington, the new method "reduced installation time considerably, because we were able to 'stuff' modules with wiring, environmental control ducting, and hydraulics before mating them. Another advantage was that we were also able to ship subassemblies by rail."

Under the old system, the MD-80 fuselages were assembled using a "clamshell" method. The top of the fuselage center section was mated with

A brand-new MD-90, resplendent in one of the individual color schemes commissioned especially for the new Japan Air Services fleet, climbs out of Tokyo's Haneda airport on a domestic flight.

two halves of the lower fuselage. Because the top fuselage section was built this way, it was too large to be transported in a single unit, so it was made on site at Long Beach. Under the new system developed for the MD-90 and later used on the MD-80, the fuselage panels were shipped from Alenia, Italy, to Long Beach. They were then taken to the McDonnell Douglas Salt Lake City facility, where they were built into three barrel sections. Each section was built with floor assemblies in place before it was shipped to Long Beach, where the sections were joined with the nose, wing, and empennage. The company hoped the new system would cut the build span from 80 days on the MD-80 to about 55 on the MD-90.

The system change involved more than moving from a clamshell method to barrels. DAC workers had to adapt to process initiatives like "just-in-time," in which parts are provided for the assembly line "just-in-time" in order to reduce wasteful inventory. The workers also had to adapt to major changes in the aircraft itself. Even though the idea was to make the MD-90 as simple a derivative as possible, the aircraft was much more than a stretch of the MD-80 with new engines. The fuselage was stretched 4 feet, 9 inches ahead of the wings, in order to balance the extra 5,900 pounds gained with the bigger engines. The resulting length was 152 feet, 7 inches, which included space for two extra seat rows and an overall seating capacity of 158.

This in turn changed the pitch inertia of the aircraft, which now required a more powerful, hydraulically operated elevator instead of the manually controlled unit used on the MD-80. In the unlikely event of a dual-hydraulic system failure, the design included manual reversion with driving tabs on the trailing edge. The elevator power control system was made by Dowty Aerospace.

Larger electrical power generators were needed on the MD-90. DAC took advantage of this requirement by introducing a variable-speed, constant-frequency (VSCF) electrical power system. Produced by Allied-Signal Aerospace's Bendix Electric Power Division, the VSCF electronically converted variable frequency power from the generators into a constant frequency. The MD-80's constant-speed drive generators were unsuitable for the higher power needs of the -90, which had a system rated at 60/75kVA. This could run for up to five minutes at 90kVA, compared with the MD-80's system, which operated at 40kVA and ran for five minutes at 60kVA. The VSCF had been designed for higher reliability, but it proved a headache to early operators like Delta until the problems were ironed out. Douglas avoided using this technology on its next project, the MD-95.

Other changes included the use of a more powerful 450-shaft horsepower APU from Allied-Signal. The 131-9D was based on the APU designed for the Northrop Grumman B-2 bomber. It was built and tested in 12 months. The MD-90 was also fitted with carbon brakes and digital anti-skid/autobrake controls.

The heavier weight was also reflected in the increased service-life goals for the airframe. The -90 had a service-life goal of 90,000 hours and 60,000 landings. By comparison, the DC-9's original goal was 30,000 hours and 40,000 landings. Although it was never launched, the MD-90-50 was designed for up to 100,000 hours but fewer landings than the -30, with 50,000 touchdowns.

Into Service

The first aircraft, T-1, made its maiden flight on February 22, 1993. It landed at Mojave, California, after a flight of four hours and 56 minutes. MD-90 program chief test pilot Bill Jones commanded the flight, with DAC test pilot Gary Smith and flight test engineer Barry McCarthy acting as crew. The second aircraft, T-2, flew three weeks ahead of schedule on August 27, 1993. It landed at DAC's flight test facility in Yuma, Arizona, after a six-hour flight.

Initial progress was swift. "Our flight rating is much higher than a lot of other programs," said Jones in May 1993. "Historically, we went back and looked at the MD-80, -87, and MD-11 programs, and we are well ahead of them. [We are] between 25 percent and 50 percent higher in initial flight rates."

The flight crew was particularly impressed with the MD-90's higher takeoff performance. "As far as engine performance on takeoff is concerned, all I can say is that it's outstanding," Jones noted. "On the -90, we have up to 28,000 pounds static thrust on each engine, compared to 19,500 pounds or 20,000 pounds on the -80. It moves down the runway, and climb rate on two engines is phenomenal. You can get 3,000 feet to 4,000 feet per minute out of it. This aeroplane really moves upstairs."

The first production MD-90 (number 3) flew on September 21, 1994, in the colors of Delta. It added a few important test hours to the 1,906 hours eventually amassed by the three aircraft in the certification effort. The FAA ticket was awarded on November 16, 1994, after a total of 1,450 flights. First official delivery to Delta followed on March 24, 1995, although the aircraft had already been operating on route-proving runs with the airline for several weeks.

Just as the first aircraft were entering airline service, McDonnell Douglas was busy renegotiating a hard-won contract with the Chinese over its Trunkliner program. This had first been secured in June 1992, after victory over a version of Boeing's 737. The original deal called for production in China of 20 MD-90-30Ts and 17 MD-80Ts. These planes would be equipped with special, four-main-wheel landing gear for low-strength Chinese runways. DAC believed the deal could eventually lead to the construction of up to 150 Trunkliners for China's rapidly expanding network.

However, the contract changed several times. By 1995, the unusual gear idea had been dropped,

and the mix of Chinese- and U.S.-built aircraft had changed. In the end, the contract called for the first of 20 Long Beach-built -90s to be handed over to Chinese airlines (China Eastern and China Northern) in 1996. No MD-80Ts were included, and the first Chinese-built aircraft was to be rolled out from the Dachang Factory of Shanghai Aviation Industrial Corporation in April 1998. Although Long Beach churned out a steady stream of MD-90s for China, the Chinese-made aircraft made almost no progress. By July 1998, parts for three aircraft were ready for assembly, but the Chinese had called a halt to the Trunkliner project.

The news for the MD-90 itself was not much better, although Saudi Arabian Airlines placed a healthy order for 29 planes as part of a multi-billion dollar contract for U.S. manufacturers arranged in 1995. Despite aggressive sales efforts and some limited success, the MD-90 simply did not sell anywhere close to the 1,000 aircraft originally predicted. Although it was technically superb and very popular with passengers for its quiet interior and comfort, the MD-90 was something of an orphan. Without sister variants and closer relatives like the early MD-XX concept, it had a hard time competing with the much broader families offered by Airbus and Boeing. One of those family members, the Boeing 737-900, finally killed off the MD-90. After the Boeing takeover in August 1997, the Seattle-based company reviewed its product strategy. Boeing also launched the almost directly competitive 737-900 in late 1997 with an order from Alaska Airlines, which had earlier canceled an MD-90 order. The handwriting was on the wall for the big twin. In November 1997, Boeing announced that it planned to phase out both the MD-80 and the MD-90, with final deliveries in 2000.

The MD-90 received a welcome boost toward the end of its production life when it was selected by Saudi Arabian Airlines to meet its standard body jet requirement. One of the 29 MD-90s ordered by Saudi is pictured here, before delivery at Long Beach. At the airline's insistence, a new glass cockpit was developed for the MD-90, using Honeywell's VIA 2000 digital avionics architecture. The same basic flightdeck design was subsequently adopted for the 717 and the MD-10.

MD-95/717:
THE LEGEND LIVES ON

Douglas' last design has one of the strangest histories of any jetliner yet developed. After struggling for survival for several years, the MD-95 competed against the newest versions of Boeing's 737. Then, unexpectedly, it became the 717, the latest member of the Boeing family. The bizarre tale of this little jetliner, which at several stages was not going to be built in Long Beach, spans the dying days of the Douglas empire and the first years of the growing Boeing dynasty.

Even though its designation, its name, and its manufacturer changed, the aircraft's design never wavered from the original goal—to build a low-cost 100-seater for the burgeoning regional jet market. From the start, the configuration was based on that of the DC-9, which had been designed to fit a similar niche. However, the roots of the 717 as a separate project go back to 1983, when DAC outlined the DC-9-90. This proposed short-body version of the MD-81 (see chapter 4) would have seated 117 passengers and was aimed at the newly deregulated U.S. market.

For many years, Northwest Airlines was the world's largest DC-9 operator. The airline became closely involved with Douglas on the -90 project which gradually evolved into a firm program. At the 1991 Paris Air Show, McDonnell Douglas, Pratt & Whitney, and the China National Aero-Technology Import Export Corporation signed a memorandum of understanding to develop a 105-seat version of the MD-80 for initial delivery in 1995. The aircraft

was briefly called the MD-87-105, but it was subsequently renamed the MD-95.

At this early stage, the MD-95 was closely linked to the MD-90 and the Chinese Trunkliner program (see chapter 6). In fact, DAC planned, at one stage, to build the MD-95 in China. In design terms, it was also more closely related to the original DC-9-90 concept than it was to the DC-9-30. DAC offered Pratt & Whitney's JT8D-218 and a proposed version of the Rolls-Royce Tay as engine options, expecting the first flight to occur in 1994.

However, like many of DAC's best ideas, the embryonic MD-95 was a victim of bad timing. The buildup of the program coincided with the Gulf War and the onset of a deep global recession. Progress was delayed by several years, but the delay resulted in one major benefit. It led to the adoption of a much more advanced engine—the BMW Rolls-Royce BR715. This advanced turbofan was to be produced from a common core developed jointly by BMW of Germany and Rolls-Royce. The BR700 series had been launched in 1991, and had subsequently been selected for two new business aircraft, the Gulfstream V and Bombardier's Global Express.

The DC-9X project replaced the MD-95 as the recession hit home and airlines looked at life-extension programs rather than the more expensive option of new equipment. The DC-9X attracted the interest of key operators such as Air Canada and Finnair, but the relatively high costs

Departing Douglas' flight test facility in Yuma, Arizona, the second 717-200 (T-2) lifts off runway 21L. This "green" aircraft is shown in its bare aluminum and composites that will soon be covered up when the aircraft is painted.

The first production 717 for launch customer AirTran comes together in Building 80, home of so many famous Douglas jetliners. The construction number, 5004, represents a last link to the days of Douglas, in that the original numbering sequence was based on the number *5* in MD-95. The previous three numbers, 5001 through 5003, were allocated to the test aircraft, T-1 to T-3.

of re-engining made the process hard to justify, so the project did not proceed. The DC-9X at least introduced the BR715 to DAC, which embraced it as the engine of choice for the MD-95 when that model re-emerged in 1994. The lessons of the DC-9X were also reflected in the MD-95, which now looked more like a DC-9-30 than a scaled-back MD-90. In fact, it was so close to the DC-9 that it had the same 119-foot, 4-inch fuselage length and the original 93-foot, 4-inch span.

Board approval for launch, given in July 1994, was based on an innovative, low-cost network of risk and revenue partners around the world. DAC's old ally, Alenia, was selected to build the fuselage. Halla (later Hyundai) of South Korea would manufacture the wings, Korean Air the nose, and British Aerospace the empennage. This tail-area work was subsequently given to Aero Industry Development Center (AIDC) of Taiwan. DAC also announced that final assembly would take place at Dalfort Aviation's site in Dallas, Texas. Final

assembly reverted to Long Beach, however, after a nationwide competition for an alternative site, hard bargaining with the unions, and concessions from California's state government. Development costs were estimated at around $500 million at the time, of which DAC's share was roughly $200 million.

In March 1995, with everything poised to launch, the program received a near-fatal blow when SAS chose the Next Generation 737-600 over the MD-95 for its new 100-seater. The DAC project teetered even closer to the brink when the exclusive supplier agreement with BMW/Rolls-Royce expired without renewal and P&W's Mid Thrust Family Engine, later called the PW6000, suddenly entered the frame. Things looked bleak until October 19, 1995, when a low-cost U.S. airline called ValuJet announced 50 orders and 50 options for BR715-powered MD-95s.

Like previous DAC products, the MD-95 came with a ready-made family from the outset. The numerous study options eventually boiled

Freshly painted in its new Boeing house colors, the prototype 717-200 T-1 presented a curious sight on the Long Beach ramp prior to its first flight in September 1998. For many, however, it was a sign of optimism that the mighty Boeing would soon inject new life into the sales efforts.

down to three main versions: a 75- to 80-seat "shrink" called the MD-95-20; a standard, 105- to 110-seat MD-95-30; and a slightly stretched 125- to 130-seat MD-95-50. All talk of these versions ground to a halt, however, following the Boeing takeover. Once more, the troubled MD-95 seemed certain to die. After all, why should Boeing allow the MD-95 to go ahead when its own 737-600, then in final development and certification phases, had recently beaten the -95 to a big order?

Whether for reasons of marketing, politics, or both, the MD-95 was destined to survive. Boeing's rigorous analysis suggested that the little twinjet was probably just what the company needed to address a regional market that was emerging *below* the smallest 737. It concurred with DAC's original forecast, which predicted a need for more than 2,500 aircraft in this size category over the next 20 years. More importantly, it provided Boeing with a ready-made weapon it could use to fight the rival Airbus A319 and the proposed A319M5 shrink, as well as potential

Asian-built Airbus models such as the AE31X. The AE31X was later abandoned in favor of the M5 shrink which was renamed the A318.

Nevertheless, Boeing's January 1998 decision to retain the MD-95 and rename it the 717 came as a huge surprise. In one sense, the move ended a product line extending back 65 years to the first delivery of the DC-1 in 1933. In another sense, Boeing had embraced the DAC product as one of its own, ensuring a massive boost of confidence in a product without many orders. The 717 model designation had first been assigned to the KC-135, a 707-based military tanker. It was given to the MD-95 because, according to Boeing, the *1* in *717* referred to the model's 100-seater capacity. Whatever the name, the DAC workforce was at least reassured that Boeing planned to support the small jetliner.

Simple Philosophy

Chief project engineer Tom Croslin was familiar with the fundamental principles behind the DC-9. "Safe, simple, and dependable—those were

The sophisticated-looking target-type thrust reverser of the BR715 engine, pictured in its fully deployed position, gleams like new before the start of the flight test program.

the three things the DC-9 was based on. We took the same approach with the 717. From the start, we had very strict rules about what changes and additions we made to the basic design. If it did not reduce recurring costs, improve dispatch reliability, reduce maintenance costs, or affect at least two of those areas, it didn't get on the aircraft," said Croslin.

The one big area of change was the tail, which had to be substantially redesigned to handle the much bigger BR715s. These engines weighed about 6,450 pounds apiece including the nacelle, compared to 4,660 pounds for the DC-9's original JT8D. Unsurprisingly, the new engines required far more structural support. This was achieved by inserting an extra frame between the existing aft frames, a better solution than trying to insert a more complex strut box in the cramped tail area. The extra frame supported the weight of the engines, while the front mounts took the thrust loads. The tail was also strengthened by using the same skin thickness that had been used in the MD-80, and the pylon used to hold the engine in place was adapted from the larger twinjet.

The tip of the vertical tail sported a slightly extended version of the MD-87-styletip, a move that increased directional stability and compensated for the shorter moment arm. The most crucial part of the balancing act was a stretch of the forward fuselage. "Originally we put in two frames, and that balanced," said Croslin. "AirTran (the former Valu-Jet) wanted another seat row, however, so we added 57 inches in all. This played us right into perfect balance, although we were a little concerned at the time that we might be making the aircraft too big. We didn't want to push ourselves onto the 737."

Externally, the wing was virtually the same as that of the heavier DC-9-34. The incidence angle was increased to 1.25 degrees, in order to replicate the -34 and increase the maximum takeoff weight to 121,000 pounds. Otherwise, the wing was identical to the -30, with an area of 1,000.7 square feet, a thickness/chord ratio of 11.6 percent, and a sweepback at quarter chord of 24 degrees.

Drag improvements originally developed for Swissair were also introduced to the wing. These included slat seals between the ribs and seals at the bottom and top of the slats. Together with a redesigned wing/fuselage fillet, the improvements gave the MD-95 a 1-percent drag reduction compared to the DC-9. The new fillet was longer and more aerodynamic, thanks to a three-bay extension. The additional structure was made from composite materials that were otherwise avoided as much as possible.

"The goal was not to use composites because the maintenance community hates it," said Croslin. "With composites, you need things like autoclaves for repairs, whereas any farm boy from Minnesota can repair a dent in aluminum with a silver dollar patch." The few remaining composite items on the aircraft included a low-drag trailing cone, the tip cap, tabs on the elevator and ailerons, the radome, and wing trailing edge panels. The only significant change in material was the use of modern 2024T3 aluminum alloy to provide greater damage tolerance and slower crack propagation properties than the 2014 alloy originally found on the DC-9.

The biggest external change was the engines. These throttled up to 25,750 pounds of thrust during tests that began in April 1997. All was going smoothly until problems cropped up with the high pressure compressor (HPC) during high-altitude tests in the United Kingdom. Cracks appeared in the third-stage HPC blades, which were based on a design used for the IAE V2500 compressor. This problem, together with others related to fan blade containment, led to a three-month delay in first flight, which finally occurred on September 1, 1998.

Changes Inside

On the outside, the 717 looked for all the world like a big-engined DC-9. On the inside, it was a different story. The flight deck was completely reworked, with MD-11 and 777-style flat panel displays operated by Honeywell's versatile integrated avionics (VIA) computers. Six liquid crystal displays, each 10 inches by 10 inches, dominated the

The design legacy of McDonnell Douglas, and particularly Douglas Aircraft, is today carried into the future with concepts like the Blended Wing Body. This highly efficient, long-range transport design is being evaluated by Boeing for potential application in the early part of the twenty-first century.

flight deck—which assumed a configuration even more advanced than the 777's. Flight control computers separate from the VIA processors gave the 717 full Category IIIa automatic landing capability. The aircraft was expected to achieve Category IIIb capability later in its lifetime, with the addition of a radio altimeter, an instrument landing system receiver, and an inertial reference unit (IRU). A later advance was the air data inertial reference unit (ADIRU), which combined the functions of the air data system and the IRU.

Another flightdeck change that instantly differentiated the 717 from the DC-9 was the absence of what DAC called "suitcase handles," as well as various other wheels, levers, and knobs. A new electrical rudder and elevator trim control system eliminated the manual aileron and rudder trim knobs, as well as the cables that ran all the way from the control pedestal to the tail. A new, electrically controlled spoiler system with a vernier control handle allowed the crew to set the speed brakes at any position without detents or latches. However, problems with the development of this system also contributed to the delay of the first flight.

All systems were brought up to date in the 717, including the primary electrical system. This system became more rugged and multiply redundant, in order to ensure that the aircraft could dispatch if one of three units failed. Other changes were made to the pneumatic and ice protection system, which bled hot air to all surfaces at the same time, and to the fuel system and air conditioning. The 717 also featured a cabin with an all-new look, designed by Fischer of Austria. It had improved lighting, larger overhead bins, new three-bay sidewall panels, and a modular lavatory with a vacuum waste system. The cabin also featured new flicker-free lighting and the full-grip handrail that had proven so successful with the introduction of the MD-90.

There were only 55 firm orders in the bag by first flight, so each and every one of these features was considered worth its weight in gold to the marketing teams that went looking for business during 1998. With hopes for a successful flight test effort and an on-time entry into service in mid-1999, marketers hoped the 717 would soon start selling in huge numbers. After all, although it now had a Boeing designation, the 717 was the last active survivor of the Douglas family. The aircraft carried with it the proud heritage of a vanished dynasty.

APPENDIX

ORDERS AND DELIVERIES, 1955–1999

Model	Variant	Delivered	Notes
DC-8	-10	28	
	-20	34	
	-30	57	
	-40	32	
	-50	143	
	-61	88	53 converted to -71
	-62	67	7 converted to -72
	-63	107	50 converted to -73
DC-9	-10	137	
	-20	10	
	-30	662	
	-40	71	
	-50	96	
DC-10	-10	131	
	-15	7	
	-30	206	
	-40	42	
KC-10A		60	
MD-80	-81	132	
	-82	562	
	-83	264*	*ordered as of 11/98
	-87	75	
	-88	158	
MD-11	Passenger	136	
	Combi	5	
	Freighter	59*	*ordered as of 1/99
MD-90	-30	134*	*ordered as of 1/99
717	-200	115*	*ordered as of 1/99

Production Totals	
DC-8	556
DC-9	976
DC-10	446
MD-80	1,191
MD-11	200
MD-90	134
717	115
Douglas Jetliner Total	3,618
	(as of January 1999)